D1055476

You have lived your faith. I commend you for your dedicated service to the ministy. Laura joins me in sending you best wishes.

—George W. Bush
(while Governor of Texas)

Mike Evans is a fighter for freedom in a world of darkening and narrowing horizons.

—Benjamin Netanyahu
Former Prime Minister of Israel

You have had the privilege of living through one of the most exciting periods of history. This thirty-year period has given you the opportunity to be a real blessing and encouragement . . . you have been a stabilizing influence and an encouragement to others who may have wavered if it had not been for your testimony and your lives.

—Billy Graham Evangelistic Association

You are an extraordinary example, dedicated to the Lord.

—Elizabeth Dole.

Only when we get to heaven will we know the full impact of the influence of your life on the lives of so many others. Thank you for your biblically-oriented, Christ-centered, Holy Spirit-empowered ministry that has had such a lasting influence on so many.

—Lloyd J. Ogilvie
Chaplain, United States Senate

You are both a testimony in your devotion and faithfulness to our Lord.

—Tim LaHaye
Coauthor, LEFT BEHIND series

I am so thankful for your example . . . your love for the Lord and commitment to His commandments is made evident by your faithfulness in His service.

—Charles Colson
Prison Fellowship Ministries

Dede joins me in sending our congratulations. God has blessed you and used you, and I thank Him for His blessing upon your ministry.

—Pat Robertson
Chairman and CEO, Christian Broadcasting Network

I am so grateful for your ceaseless, lifelong committed devotion to spreading the Word! You both are a blessing from the Lord to all of us.

—Dr. Robert Schuller
Senior Pastor, The Crystal Cathedral

It is with great joy that we send our love, prayers, and congratulations to you for the many years of unselfish sacrifice that you have given in our ministry. What an awesome result of the work you are rendering in the kingdom. You are a great asset among the body of believers that work in the vineyard.

—Bishop T. D. Jakes
The Potter's House, Dallas, Texas,
and T. D. Jakes Ministries

To God be the glory for all He has accomplished through your dedicated lives! We are certain the Lord will have a great reward for you when you stand before His throne. Through all the highs and lows, the testing and blesssings, you have both proven to be solid and faithful to the ways of the Lord. Now your many friends rise up to give thanks to the Lord for your faithfulness. We are glad to be counted among your friends.

—David Wilkerson
Times Square Church

From your firm commitment to spread the Gospel worldwide to your efforts to honor Christian leaders, your deep love for God is so evident and inspiring.

—Dr. James and Shirley Dobson
Focus on the Family

The Un-Answered Prayers of Jesus

MIKE EVANS

BETHANYHOUSE
PUBLISHERS
MINNEAPOLIS, MINNESOTA

Library of Congress Cataloging-in-Publication Data

Evans, Mike, 1947-
    The unanswered prayers of Jesus / by Mike Evans.
        p.   cm.
Includes bibliographical references.
    ISBN 0-7642-2757-2 (alk. paper)
    1. Christian life.   2. Jesus Christ—Prayers.   I. Title.
BV4509.5.E84   2003
248.4—dc21   2003001872

Dedicated to

. . . those who are willing to pay any price

until Jesus is so fully manifested in their lives

that the shadow they cast is not theirs

but the shadow of Jesus,

which causes a lost world to follow them with a dying passion,

knowing that they have

"been with Jesus."

. . . to those whose heart's cry is

"Less of me, all of Him."

About the Author

Mike Evans is an award-winning journalist, producer, and minister. Millions throughout the world have seen the television specials he has hosted. Evans' prime-time television specials have received national awards on thirteen different occasions and have included guests Kathie Lee Gifford, Evander Holyfield, Deion Sanders, Steve Allen, Gavin MacLeod, James Garner, Pat Boone, Monty Hall, and Jayne Meadows. Evans has been a personal confidant to numerous world leaders.

As a writer, he has been published in the *Wall Street Journal, Newsweek,* and numerous other publications. He is a member of the National Press Club. Evans has covered world events for more than two decades.

He has appeared on hundreds of radio and television broadcasts, including *Good Morning, America, Nightline, Crossfire, The Good Morning Show* (Great Britain), *The 700 Club* (Christian Broadcasting Network), *Praise the Lord!* (Trinity Broadcasting Network), and the Salem Broadcasting Network. NBC, ABC, CBS, Fox Broadcasting Network, and CNN World News have covered him.

As a public speaker, Evans has spoken to more than four thousand audiences throughout the world. In the United States, he has spoken at the Orange Bowl, Giants Stadium, and Arrowhead Stadium. In the 1990s alone, he addressed more than ten million people face to face around the globe, with more than 110,000 ministers attending his conferences.

Mike Evans' wife, Carolyn, is Chairwoman and Founder of the Christian Woman of the Year Association. Ruth Graham, Elizabeth Dole, Mother Teresa, and other distinguished women are among the recipients who have been honored over the past fifteen years. The executive committee is comprised of a number of prominent women, including Dr. Cory SerVaas, owner of the *Saturday Evening Post.*

Contents

Introduction

In the mid-1980s I was rushing through an airport in Rome with a friend of mine, a television producer, when I spotted at the opposite end of the terminal a short, stooped woman wearing a familiar robe.

"Paul," I told my friend, "watch our stuff." I threw my bags at his feet and ran to meet her.

"My name is Mike Evans," I said as I approached, offering my hand to shake hers. Mother Teresa's dark eyes twinkled up at me as she grasped my outstretched hand and said, "Mike Evans, it is very nice to meet you."

All the love of the universe seemed to drain from the atmosphere at that moment. It was as if it concentrated within her tiny frame and radiated through her. My flight and my friend no longer existed. Like a schoolboy, I stammered a few words about my current mission to Israel, then collected myself and asked about her recent trip to the United States. I thought I would sympathize with her for returning to the suffering in India after enjoying the comforts of the States for a short time.

"No, no," she responded with a sad smile. "It is in the United States that I am sad. I believe it is the poorest country on earth."

"But why?" I asked, stumbling in my attempt at small talk with this giant of the faith.

"Ah," she went on. "The United States is poor in spirit, and that is the worst kind of poverty."

I have meditated on Mother Teresa's profound statement in the years since that encounter, and I have come to understand it more each day. In a land of wealth and opulence, with every opportunity afforded us—from timesaving gadgets to life-enhancing luxuries—our nation as a whole seems devoid of true fulfillment and lasting contentment. Even with all of our computer-age technology, state-of-the-art communications satellites, multimillion-dollar universities, and Internet-ready cell phones, we still don't seem able to rise to a level of greatness equal to our level of wealth. Like a good dream that doesn't last until morning, personal peace is fleeting, and achieving a fulfilling purpose for living eludes us. We seem a nation of people who struggle to know divine destiny, settling instead for complacency.

Yet within our hearts destiny still calls. Somehow we know we were meant for something greater than what we are now living, but we are not sure what it is or how to start experiencing it.

Some of Jesus Christ's final words as He left this earth were, "All power in heaven and in earth is given to me. So go and make followers of all people in the world. . . . I will be with you always."[1] He also promised that Christians would do "greater works" than He did because He went "unto the Father."[2] He promised that signs and wonders would follow His believers.[3] One of the most puzzling parts of becoming a Christian today is to read those promises yet not experience any of them in our own lives. This is spiritual poverty.

New Christians are initially excited about their newfound faith, eager to seek God's favor and will for their lives. Now that they know there is a God and that He is the One who created the entire universe, they read their Bibles hoping to live every passage in it. For a while many do live in this power and can never imagine doing anything but what God has set before them. But then other concerns and desires begin to creep in, and they are stymied. Somehow they meet disappointment in something they were hoping for, and they start making excuses. They look around themselves in the church and settle in to the "norm" they have experienced there, measuring spirituality by those they see around them. They begin to slowly forget or explain away the life of the supernatural they thought they had signed up for when they first pledged to follow Christ. They simply settle for less. Again, this is spiritual poverty.

Yet the promises and prayers of Jesus don't call us to live lives marked by such mediocrity and impotence. His prayers for His followers are that their lives will be marked by the intimacy of His relationship with His Father and alive with the works of His Spirit. If Jesus prayed this, wouldn't you think it should be coming to pass in our lives?

After all, no one in history is credited with answering more prayers than Jesus Christ. During His earthly ministry, the most amazing answers to prayer were recorded: from people born blind receiving their sight to the disabled suddenly walking and leaping—even the dead being raised back to life again. Since His crucifixion, millions have testified to having their prayers answered by calling on His name. His is still the largest movement ever birthed on the planet, with roughly two billion followers today. However, *written plainly in the ancient texts of the Bible are prayers that were prayed by Jesus himself that have never been answered.* Is there some connection between this and our spiritual poverty?

On the night before His crucifixion, Jesus gathered His disciples in an upper room in Jerusalem to be in their company one last evening and prepare them for what lay ahead. John, in chapters 13–17, recorded the events that took place in that room, and this passage is among the greatest sections of teaching in the Bible. Jesus ended that evening with a prayer not only for those with Him at that time, "but for them also which shall believe on me through their [the disciples'] word."[4] In this prayer are nine specific requests that have never fully come to pass in the lives of Christ's disciples or in the generations that have followed their words: They remain unfulfilled today. Why did the very One who is considered the source of answered prayer leave with some of His own prayers unanswered? Will they be answered? If so, when? How? And by whom?

I have asked myself these questions over and over in my more than three decades of ministry. During that time God has taken me around the world and before great leaders. I have seen God do incredible things. I have experienced the spiritual poverty Mother Teresa spoke of, but I have also experienced the spiritual abundance those in the book of Acts lived out through simple obedience. I have seen God heal the sick and disabled, miraculously open doors to high officials in major governments, and use me and others to work His will in ways I could never have imagined possible. If I have read my Bible correctly, these incredible things shouldn't be unusual in the path of those who follow Christ: They are the works every believer is called to do according to the Scriptures. Even so, only a few believers I have known have left such signs and wonders in their wakes. It is my belief that the answers to the points in Jesus' prayer in John 17 will only be realized when more of us rise up to walk in this spiritual abundance and are unwilling to settle for the spiritual lack that seems to grip most of Western Christianity. Are we willing to set aside our complacency to be part of the answer to Jesus' prayers?

Though Christian denominations differ on many points of faith, there seems to be one thing we share in common: We all believe that God answers prayers. Yet if there are prayers prayed by God's own Son that have gone unanswered, how can any of us have confidence in the prayers we offer Him? The fact that Jesus Christ had unanswered prayers is either the greatest challenge to the faith of Christians today or it is the greatest mystery in the Bible—and in its solving are the greatest keys to living a supernatural life we could hope to have, keys out of spiritual poverty and into the fullness of Christ.[5]

I don't know about you, but that's the type of life I want to live—a life that will be part of the solution to that mystery and an answer to Jesus' unanswered prayers. That's the Christian life I signed up for and, by God's grace, it is the life I have experienced too often to settle for anything less.

Mike Evans
Bedford, Texas

CHAPTER ONE

What We Signed Up For

All power is given unto me in heaven and in earth. Go ye therefore,
and teach all nations. . . . I am with you alway, even unto the end
of the world.

MATTHEW 28:18–20

Go ye into all the world, and preach the gospel to every creature. . . .
And these signs shall follow them that believe; in my name shall they
cast out devils; they shall speak with new tongues . . . they shall lay
hands on the sick, and they shall recover.

MARK 16:15, 17–18

I will never forget the day I first received an inkling of what Jesus
wanted to do in my life. I even remember the time. It was 2:25
P.M. on October 19, 1967. I know that because I was looking at
the clock behind the head of Professor Harris while sitting in his
office at the Bible college I attended.

I was a frustrated young man, and I could not understand
what God wanted from my life. Because of my Jewish background, I'd risked my relationship with my family in order to
become a Christian, and now there didn't seem to be anything to
do as a Christian. I was suffering from spiritual poverty and didn't
even know it.

"I don't like church," I told him. That's all I could figure out that was wrong. I'd sat through lessons, gone to Bible studies, and attended services every time one was held, but I was still deeply dissatisfied in my heart. *Is this all there is to being a Christian?*

I talked a bit more with Professor Harris as I fumbled to better explain myself. At the end of my voicing my dissatisfaction with much of what I had experienced so far, he advised me, "You better think twice about going into the ministry! Let's pray."

As we bowed to pray, immediately the Lord reminded me, "If two or more shall agree as touching any one thing, I will do it."[1] Realizing this was an opportunity for such an agreement in prayer, I decided to hold nothing back. I surrendered all of my life to Christ in a way I'd never done before.

> *I knew that after all I had risked to enlist as one of Christ's soldiers, I could never simply fill a vacancy in the pew of my local church.*

When my beloved professor and I finished, he said, "Mike, just find a church and be faithful."

I left nodding my head but also determining in my heart to do much more with Christ's promises than just being faithful to a local church.

Perhaps in expressing my dissatisfaction with all I had experienced of the Christian life in his office that day, I realized, without my professor's knowledge, that if all I ever did was hear about Christ's power and never experience it, I would be forever disillusioned—a condition many Christians find themselves in today. I knew that after all I had risked to enlist as one of Christ's soldiers, I could never simply fill a vacancy in the pew of my local church and feel like I'd accomplished anything at all. I became aware that He died for much more than my privilege to sit in church, sing a few songs, and listen to some make-you-feel-better sermons. I wanted to do what I'd signed up for—to live a life like Jesus lived!

Time for a Reality Check

Anyone who reads the Gospels realizes that, for the great majority of Christians today, we are experiencing very little of what happened regularly during the life and ministry of Jesus. Then if you go on to read the book of Acts, you have to question what the church did to unplug itself from the power it walked in during those times. Miracles and visions were a regular part of first-century Christianity. Why aren't we living like that today?

Many have said that it is simply because God ordained miracles for that era, and now we are living in a different time, or dispensation, of God's activity, when we need to have faith without seeing miracles. That seems to make sense if you look at circumstances today. In fact, it makes many wish they had lived in the times of Jesus so that they might get the help they need. If we could just see Jesus—if we could just touch Him—everything would be better. If we could just walk with Jesus as the disciples did, then maybe we would also have the power of God available to us the way it was available to them. The reason we don't experience the help we need is that things are different today, since Jesus is no longer walking the earth as He did with the disciples.

Yet if you read what Jesus himself said to His disciples on the night before He was crucified, you realize that things today are different but not in the ways we have traditionally thought. Jesus never said anything about the miracles He performed being just for that time or there being different eras of God's grace. In fact, Jesus told His disciples that God had much more power for them to walk in *after He left* than what they were experiencing as they walked with Him during His earthly ministry.

How can I say this? Because Jesus himself told them, "It is better for you that I go away."[2] He also said, "He that believeth on me, the works that I do shall he do also; and greater works than these shall he do; *because I go unto my Father*."[3] There were no time limits set on this. It was something that those who believed on Him would experience, and *it wouldn't happen until after He ascended.*

Look again at what Jesus said to His disciples at the end of the book of Matthew:

> All power is given unto me in heaven and in earth. Go ye therefore, and teach all nations, baptizing them in the name of the Father, and of the Son, and of the Holy Ghost: Teaching them to observe all things whatsoever I have commanded you: and, lo, I am with you alway, even unto the end of the world. (Matthew 28:18–20)

Many of you are familiar with this passage, called the Great Commission, Jesus' instructions to His disciples—and to us— that we take the gospel to the ends of the earth before He comes again. How many of us have heard this passage quoted to us in sermons about evangelism or missions and been told that this is God's commandment to us to tell others about Jesus? No one ever says in this connection that the age of evangelism has passed away, but then we, through the doctrine of dispensationalism, deny the power He speaks of—we deny the very basis and implication of the Scripture: "All the power of heaven and earth has been given to me, *therefore you go* and make disciples . . . because I—and all of that power given to me—will always be with you, even until the end of the world." Doesn't this imply that it is *because* we have the power of God with us that we should go and make disciples, and not that we should go and make disciples without it?

Mark records this in a similar way:

> Go ye into all the world, and preach the gospel to every creature. He that believeth and is baptized shall be saved; but he that believeth not shall be damned. And these signs shall follow them that believe; in my name shall they cast out devils; they shall speak with new tongues; they shall take up serpents; and if they drink any deadly thing, it shall not hurt them; they shall lay hands on the sick, and they shall recover. (Mark 16:15–18)

In other words, miraculous signs—devils cast out, people speaking in languages foreign to them, poisonous serpents being shaken off without harm,[4] and attempts made on the lives of His followers having no effect on them—would follow those that believed on Jesus' name.

Why is this? Jesus made it plain on that night before His crucifixion:

> I will pray the Father, and he shall give you another Comforter, that he may abide with you for ever. . . . These things have I spoken unto you, being yet present with you. But the Comforter, which is the Holy Ghost, whom the Father will send in my name, he shall teach you all things, and bring all things to your remembrance, whatsoever I have said unto you. (John 14:16, 25–26)
>
> I tell you the truth; it is expedient for you that I go away: for if I go not away, the Comforter will not come unto you; but if I depart, I will send him unto you. (John 16:7)

While Jesus was on the earth, He had the Spirit of God, the Holy Spirit, without measure[5]—all the power of God and His wisdom wrapped up in one Man in one place—but once He ascended, the Holy Spirit would then live in the hearts of all believers around the world. The implication is not only that the disciples would be better off when Jesus left but also that those who believe on Jesus because of their preaching would also be better off than when Jesus walked on the earth. If we had walked with Jesus as His disciples did, we would have had access to the power of God whenever we were with Him, just like the woman with the issue of blood received her wholeness when she touched the hem of his garment;[6] but now that He has ascended to the right hand of the Father, we have that same power of God within each of us in the person of the Holy Spirit. This is how we are to walk in the "greater works"—through the Holy Spirit who lives inside every believer.

Has the Holy Spirit gone away? No. And this being the case,

it would be logical also to say that neither have the works He did through Jesus and the disciples. If the Holy Spirit is still here in our time as He was in theirs, then the gifts of the Holy Spirit that they walked in must still be with us as well.

But if this is true, why aren't we experiencing these gifts as they did? When was the last time any of us experienced this miracle-working power? It would seem logical to assume that something has changed, because we don't see the miracles Jesus and the disciples manifested anymore.

> *Somehow, in spite of myself, I have stumbled again and again into Jesus operating the same today as He did when He walked the earth.*

I might well have agreed with those that say miracles are not for today, had my simple hunger for more of God—my dissatisfaction with the status quo—not led me, rather by accident, to experiences that tell me Jesus' words haven't changed over the centuries. Somehow, in spite of myself, I have stumbled again and again into Jesus operating the same today as He did when He walked the earth. This has led me to see that for those who will make themselves available, the Holy Spirit will work just the same today as He has in every century since Jesus ascended to heaven.

God Wants to Work Through You As He Did Through Jesus

On one occasion in Lake Charles, Louisiana, in the late 1970s, I was asked to hold a one-night crusade. This was after several weeks of travel, which had left me absolutely exhausted. A little girl with blue eyes, blond pigtails, and a bag on her lap sat in the front row. Her leg bones were so bowed that her feet were twisted upward, and she had to walk on her ankles.

Before she came that night, she had learned I was Jewish, which in her mind made me just like Jesus. Before the service, she insisted her mother buy her a new pair of pink shoes to take to the meeting so she'd have shoes to wear after her feet were healed. In the bag on her lap were the shoes.

I had never witnessed a healing from such a severe deformity in any of my services. Did I have enough power or faith to see her healed? What if I disappointed her when she evidently had such faith? At the close of the meeting, I prayed for everyone in the building and left her for last, hoping many in the congregation would have left. They didn't.

Finally, I picked her up and placed her on a little table next to me. I was so afraid of what was not going to happen that I closed my eyes as tightly as I could and at first silently prayed, *God, I'm so exhausted, and I don't feel like I have an ounce of faith*. My flesh, which had already assumed full responsibility, was telling me, *You're too tired to sense the Holy Spirit. Nothing is going to happen. You're going to be embarrassed. She'll go away disappointed.*

Yet I prayed, asking God for her healing. As I was praying, I began to hear people screaming and crying. I thought, *This is surely compassion for this little girl*. I didn't open my eyes because I was afraid to look. Suddenly, the pastor shook my arm, saying, "Open your eyes, open your eyes, and see what God has done!"

When I did open my eyes, there in front of me was the little girl wearing her new pair of pink shoes. Her ankles and legs were straight and normal.

Why had I thought it had anything to do with me? The little girl had the faith, and God was the miracle worker—not me. What a lesson I learned that evening as I fell to my knees and asked God to forgive me for thinking I had any power to heal.

Jamie Buckingham, a journalist and friend, invited me to join him on an eleven-day trip to the Sinai Desert to retrace the footsteps of Moses. On the sixth day, we came upon a Bedouin family. The Arab woman had heard that a doctor, Angus Sargeant, was in our group. As we approached the encampment, the woman ran to us in tears, clutching her child in her arms. The little six-year-old girl had fallen into a fire, and approximately one-third of her head was covered with a huge abscess. As a result, she was burning up with fever and in great pain. As the woman begged the doctor for medicine, he turned to us and said, "This is a hopeless situation. I have no medicine that I can give the child. She needs surgery, or she may die."

We learned that others in the Bedouin camp had taken hot knives to the child's face in an attempt to kill the infection. Instead, the little girl's face had been terribly scarred. As I thought of my own three precious daughters, the compassion of Christ came upon me. I reached out my hand and placed it on that green abscess, covered with flies. I began to intercede earnestly for this mother's daughter.

In the natural, nothing happened. We left the camp and headed toward Mount Sinai. Angus turned to the group and said, "I must go back. I have to operate on that child and try to save her." A professional photographer in our group, Skip Jones, had taken a picture of the little girl. He decided to return with Angus and me. Angus entered the tent, and within a few moments, we could hear him crying. Skip and I peeked into the tent and saw Angus with a rusty cup filled with polluted water. As the Arab mother wept, he had lifted the cup to Jesus and was praying, "Lord, I don't want to offend this woman by not drinking from the cup she has offered me. It is all she has." The offering she had given to Angus was her best offering. It was her expression of gratitude, for by her side was the same little girl—except there was no abscess, and there were no scars. The child had been completely and miraculously healed. Angus did not have to operate. Skip took a second picture of the child, and we leapt for joy and blessed the Lord for His mercy and compassion.

Through such experiences, I began to realize that Jesus had other intentions for the way His church should operate in this day and age. His plan was not that we would be so defeated and despondent that the world would look down on us—that we would be so full of spiritual poverty that you couldn't tell us from those in the world who live without hope.

Jesus' Prayers for *All* His Followers

The best passage I have found that describes how Jesus wanted us to live in the age following His ascension, what many call the church age—the time between His ascension and His second coming—is the prayer He prayed for His disciples in John 17. Take a moment to read this passage and see if any of it sounds like what you are experiencing in your life and your church gatherings:

> These words spake Jesus, and lifted up his eyes to heaven, and said, Father, the hour is come; glorify thy Son, that thy Son also may glorify thee: As thou hast given him power over all flesh, that he should give eternal life to as many as thou hast given him. And this is life eternal, that they might know thee the only true God, and Jesus Christ, whom thou hast sent. I have glorified thee on the earth: I have finished the work which thou gavest me to do. And now, O Father, glorify thou me with thine own self with the glory which I had with thee before the world was.
>
> I have manifested thy name unto the men which thou gavest me out of the world: thine they were, and thou gavest them me; and they have kept thy word. Now they have known that all things whatsoever thou hast given me are of thee. For I have given unto them the words which thou gavest me; and they have received them, and have known surely that I came out from thee, and they have believed that thou didst send me. I pray for them: I pray not for the world, but for them which thou hast given me; for they are thine. And all mine are thine, and thine are mine; and I am glorified in them.
>
> And now I am no more in the world, but these are in the world, and I come to thee. Holy Father, keep through thine own name those whom thou hast given me, that they may be one, as we are. While I was with them in the world, I kept them in thy name: those that thou gavest me I have kept, and none of them is lost, but the son of perdition; that the scripture might be fulfilled. And now come I to thee; and these things I speak in the world, that they might

have my joy fulfilled in themselves. I have given them thy word; and the world hath hated them, because they are not of the world, even as I am not of the world. I pray not that thou shouldest take them out of the world, but that thou shouldest keep them from the evil. They are not of the world, even as I am not of the world.

Sanctify them through thy truth: thy word is truth. As thou hast sent me into the world, even so have I also sent them into the world. And for their sakes I sanctify myself, that they also might be sanctified through the truth.

Neither pray I for these alone, but for them also which shall believe on me through their word; That they all may be one; as thou, Father, art in me, and I in thee, that they also may be one in us: that the world may believe that thou hast sent me. And the glory which thou gavest me I have given them; that they may be one, even as we are one: I in them, and thou in me, that they may be made perfect in one; and that the world may know that thou hast sent me, and hast loved them, as thou hast loved me.

Father, I will that they also, whom thou hast given me, be with me where I am; that they may behold my glory, which thou hast given me: for thou lovedst me before the foundation of the world. O righteous Father, the world hath not known thee: but I have known thee, and these have known that thou hast sent me. And I have declared unto them thy name, and will declare it: that the love wherewith thou hast loved me may be in them, and I in them. (John 17:1–26)

How is it that Jesus' own prayers could go unanswered?

In studying this passage, I have found nine particular points (which are discussed in the following nine chapters) that Jesus prayed that are *not coming to pass in the lives of believers today*—nine prayers that are unanswered.

In this passage, Jesus is praying for His disciples, but in verse 20 He says, "Neither pray I for these alone, but for them also which shall believe on me through their word." Thus believers in all the centuries following are included in this prayer, because we are those who have believed on Christ through the word and testimony of the disciples. *When Jesus prayed for His disciples in John 17, He was also praying for us.*

How is it that Jesus' own prayers could go unanswered?

Before we discuss this, let's look at what they were:

(1) That we would know the only true God[7]
(2) That we would be one as He and His Father are one[8]
(3) That we would have His joy[9]
(4) That we would be kept from evil[10]
(5) That we would be sanctified through the truth[11]
(6) That we would behold His glory[12]
(7) That we would be made perfect[13]
(8) That the world would know that we have been with Jesus,[14] and
(9) That the love of God would be released to the world through us.[15]

In spits and spurts these prayers have been partially answered from time to time and in individual lives, but Jesus was praying for His body as a whole, the church—not the church on the corner, the Catholic Church, the Baptist, Methodist, charismatic, or any other specific denomination (First Assembly, Faith Community, or whatever other individual congregation that we may belong to), but the universal church of all who have called upon the name of Jesus to be saved.

Can we with any honesty say that these prayers have been fully answered when we look at Christians today? Do we know God? Are we one? Are we perfect? Do we pour forth His joy, His love, or His glory? You have to admit that the church on the earth today is a far cry from the "glorious church, not having spot, or wrinkle, or any such thing"[16] that He plans to come back for. Somehow either God has refused to answer Jesus' prayers or else

His body on the earth has failed to hook up with His will for its life.

As I have studied these unanswered prayers, I have come to realize that it is a case of the latter: These prayers cannot be answered without our cooperation. Because of God's gift of free will, God's own desires for us do not take precedence over our own wills for our lives.

Perhaps the best example of this is how God wills that all be saved[17]: Are they all then automatically saved? No! They have to make their own choice whether to accept Jesus as Lord and Savior or not. It is with their own mouth that they have to confess Jesus as Lord and with their own heart that they must believe God raised Him from the dead in order for them to be saved.[18] I can't do that for them; their mother can't do that for them; and even God himself can't do it for them. We have the choice of whether or not to connect with what God has already provided. It is just as if I went to the store and bought a present for my wife and took it home and gave it to her. Though it is bought and paid for and truly belongs to her, she will never have it until she decides to unwrap the box and accept the gift.

God's will for our lives is the same way. Jesus paid for our salvation in all areas through the Cross, but unless we are willing to receive it, we will never have it. No matter how much our hearts cry out to have His will accomplished in our lives, unless we take the action to receive it according to His Word, we will never have it.

When I first realized all of this, I suddenly began to better understand the dissatisfaction I had expressed in my professor's office. My heart was crying out for God's will for my life, expressing dissatisfaction in conforming to the world's way of living and thinking for how one should become a believer. My heart told me that there had to be something more, but I didn't know what.

Then when I further realized that Christ had pray
not yet been fulfilled, and that if I would make myse_
Him I could be instrumental in their being fulfilled, I received _
sense of destiny that gave my life new purpose and meaning. Suddenly divine truth penetrated to the core of my being, and my
life mattered! The purpose for my life—and for the life of every
Christian on this earth—is to stand in agreement with our Lord
and Savior for His prayers to be answered, just as I stood in agreement with His will that I be saved.

What revelation!

It was as if a giant vacuum started to clean me out—the clouds
of confusion vanished from my mind, and the burdensome
"oughts" and "shoulds" flew off my shoulders. All I had to do
was pray in agreement with Christ, then walk in agreement with
His Spirit, and see His prayers answered in the world around me!
I realized that when Christians come together (in what we traditionally call church) under Christ's lordship with a sense of divine
desperation to see His prayers answered, it is a point in the spirit
realm where heaven and earth meet, where the mind of Christ
can be revealed and the power of Christ manifested.

This is the answer to every person's identity, destiny, inferior-
ity, or insecurity. We have purpose, we have meaning, we have
destiny, because all of Christ's prayers are not yet answered! What
we have to do is pay attention to Christ's prayers and be obedient
to His direction regarding how to fulfill them!

Jesus Wants *You*!

The disciples did have an advantage: They had been with Jesus
and seen His Father's will work through Him every day for at least
three years. When He left them, and they received the Holy Spirit
on the day of Pentecost, they had a living example of how to walk
in what they had received. Yet if the truth were told, the greatest
among them had never experienced any of that!

And who was this? Paul. Paul did not walk around Israel
watching Jesus heal the sick, cast out demons, and raise the dead.

Perhaps that is why he is the one that left us the most explicit instructions for living the Christian life, having written more letters that became part of the New Testament than any of the others. I wouldn't doubt if he also more diligently read the Gospels about Jesus than any of the rest, because they had experienced these stories firsthand and he hadn't. We certainly don't have the experiences that the disciples had of walking with Jesus, but we do have the same resources that Paul had. He simply read what the others had written and believed—then walked in as much (if not more) of the power of God.

It is time for us to do the same. We need to read what these men of God wrote about Jesus and simply believe it, tossing out whatever else others have told us that we are to expect. God will not contradict His Word, but He will confirm it with signs.[19]

It is time for us to hook up with what Jesus prayed for us.

CHAPTER TWO

Jesus, My Lord and My Friend

That they might know thee the only true God, and Jesus Christ,
whom thou hast sent.

JOHN 17:3

God, I'm hungry. I want to know you. Will you use me?"

Such were my prayers in Jerusalem on February 17, 1993.
The funny thing is that this was not at the beginning of my Christian walk or even the beginning of my ministry. I was already well
established, and my ministry was doing quite well. I had been to
the White House to serve on advisory boards made up of ministers, I had been on national talk shows, I was speaking regularly
and met frequently with world leaders. *My* ministry was going
fine. The problem was that it was not my ministry I wanted to do
anymore but *Jesus'* ministry.

I had come to realize that I knew a lot about Jesus and could
talk about Him for hours, but *I didn't really know Him.* Here I
was trying to serve Jesus with all of *my* mind and *my* strength, and
I was failing because *I didn't even know Him!* At that point I was
desperate to change this—and, as He always does, God began to
answer this desperate prayer.

Do We Know Jesus, or Only Know About Him?

In John 17:3, Jesus prayed that we "might know thee the only true God, and Jesus Christ, whom thou hast sent." Yet most Christians today seem content to go through life with what they or someone else *thinks* about God rather than truly *knowing* Him for themselves. The truth of the matter is, most of us are content to go to church and hear about God, His Son, and His Holy Spirit, but if He were ever to ask us to meet with Him personally, we would be too terrified to go!

> *I had come to realize that I knew a lot about Jesus and could talk about Him for hours, but I didn't really know Him.*

When Israel had been led out of Egypt by Moses, had escaped safely by passing through the Red Sea, and had seen in the desert God's miraculous provision of manna and quail, and water from a rock, you would think they knew God well—but, in fact, *they still refused to draw near to Him!* Even though they had seen Moses ascend the mountain and come back unharmed, his face glowing with the glory of the Lord, they chose to have someone else between them and God at all times; they feared knowing Him personally. Moses recorded it this way:

> And it came to pass, when ye heard the voice out of the midst of the darkness, (for the mountain did burn with fire,) that ye came near unto me, even all the heads of your tribes, and your elders; And ye said, Behold, the LORD our God hath shewed us his glory and his greatness, and we have heard his voice out of the midst of the fire: we have seen this day that God doth talk with man, and he liveth.
>
> *Now therefore why should we die?* for this great fire will consume us: if we hear the voice of the LORD our God any more, then we shall die. For who is there of all flesh, that hath heard the voice of the living God speaking out of the midst of the fire, as we have, and lived? *Go thou near,* and hear all that the LORD our God shall say: and speak

thou unto us all that the LORD our God shall speak unto thee; and we will hear it, and do it. (Deuteronomy 5:23–27)

In other words, though they knew of God's greatness, of His miracle-working power to deliver, and had heard Him speak from the cloud and the mountaintop, they still did not want to get too close to Him. They said, "Go *thou* near"—in other words, "Moses, you go and talk to God. You go and find out His plans. Then come tell us. We will do whatever He wants, but we just don't want to have to get close to Him."

Are we really any different today? We flock to churches to do what? Hear from God? Heavens no! We flock to church to hear others tell us what they have learned about God. "Well, my pastor says . . ." or "Well, such-and-such a minister said the other day . . ." or "I read in this book . . ." But take time to get on our knees and enter the Holy of Holies? Get our instructions from God firsthand? Draw near and get to know God and His nature for ourselves? Can we really do that?

Don't get me wrong—learning from pastors, teachers, traveling ministers, and elders in your church is important—but are you adding their teachings to the knowledge of God you have attained through time spent with Him, or are they your sole source of information?

One of our biggest hindrances to knowing God is that we don't really believe we can know Him. Think about it. The Bible is filled with offers from God that we could *know* Him if we are just willing to draw near, but do you know God even as well as some of your acquaintances? Is He the first person you think of to go to for advice, a loan, or to shoot the breeze over coffee or a bagel? How well do we—any of us—really know God?

> *One of our biggest hindrances to knowing God is that we don't really believe we can know Him.*

Jesus Came to a People Who No Longer Knew God

When Jesus began His ministry on the earth, He was constantly confronted by religious leaders who had the same Old Testament offers to know God that we have today but who chose rather to live in what they thought and deduced about God rather than drawing near to truly know Him personally. They spent more time in their Bible commentaries, the ones they used to explain God and His laws, than in the Scriptures themselves! They didn't seek God individually or corporately, and they spent little time studying His actual Word to them. Instead they sat and listened to men debate their own opinions about God until they were so far removed from God's heart that they were ready to condemn *God himself*, in the person of Jesus, as a heretic and a blasphemer when He came to them! Think about it: Throughout history, how many have been condemned by the church itself when, in fact, they were leading people back to true worship, true religion, and a true relationship with God?

When Jesus returns for His bride, the church, will it be a bride who doesn't know Him?

God forbid! Instead, the Scriptures say,

> Christ also loved the church, and gave himself for it;
> That he might sanctify and cleanse it with the washing of
> water by the word, That he might present it to himself a
> glorious church, not having spot, or wrinkle, or any such
> thing; but that it should be holy and without blemish.
> (Ephesians 5:24–27)

Could this possibly be a church that knows Him as little as we do today?

Can We Be Friends With God?

God has always revealed himself to those who truly wanted to know Him—and such people were called the friends of God.

The Bible says of Abraham:

Abraham believed God, and it was imputed unto him for righteousness: and he was called *the Friend of God.* (James 2:23)

Art not thou our God, who didst drive out the inhabitants of this land before thy people Israel, and gavest it to the seed of *Abraham thy friend* for ever? (2 Chronicles 20:7)

Why was Abraham called God's friend? He was a man who communicated with God directly, cutting a covenant with him through the blood sacrifice of animals[1] and circumcision,[2] pleading for the people of Sodom and Gomorrah,[3] and obedient even to the death of his own son.[4] He was a man who knew God through direct contact with Him, and he became the father of two covenants,

> *God has always revealed himself to those who truly wanted to know Him—and such people were called the friends of God.*

both the old covenant to the Jews and the new covenant to all believers, because his willingness to sacrifice his own son for God was the precursor of God's willingness to sacrifice his own Son for humankind. Abraham knew God through a one-on-One relationship where there was mutual respect and dedication— Abraham knew God personally by spending time with Him continually.

Look what the Bible says of Jacob, the man who wrestled with God until he received His blessing:

And he [God] said, Thy name shall be called no more Jacob, but Israel: for as a prince hast thou power with God and with men, and hast prevailed. . . . And Jacob called the name of the place Peniel: for I have seen God face to face, and my life is preserved. (Genesis 32:28, 30)

It was through coming face to face with God that Jacob came to know God and have power with God and men.

Look at what the Bible says about Moses:

> And the LORD spake unto Moses face to face, as a man speaketh unto his friend. (Exodus 33:11)

Why was this? Look at the desires of Moses' heart as expressed in this prayer that appears just a few verses later:

> I pray thee, if I have found grace in thy sight, show me now thy way, *that I may know thee,* that I may find grace in thy sight: and consider that this nation is thy people. . . . If thy presence go not with me, carry us not up hence. For wherein shall it be known here that I and thy people have found grace in thy sight? is it not in that thou goest with us? so shall we be separated, I and thy people, from all the people that are upon the face of the earth. . . . *I beseech thee, show me thy glory.* (Exodus 33:13, 15–16, 18)

According to *Vine's Complete Expository Dictionary of Old and New Testament Words,* " 'To know' God is to have an intimate experiential knowledge of Him."[5] Again, Moses knew God because he had experienced Him personally.

Many think that knowing God is a privilege of a chosen few Abrahams, Moseses, Davids, or Pauls, selected as representatives of their generations. In reality, these were men who waited on God, men who spent tremendous times alone in prayer with Him, men whose hearts desired fervently to know God. And it has always been to people like these, with such uncompromisingly desperate hearts, to whom God has revealed himself.

Getting to Know Him

This may sound somewhat mystical, but don't complicate the matter. If you really want to know Jesus, then it is not much different than getting to know another person. If we wanted to get to know a famous person, for example, we would perhaps first read about him. *We have the story of Jesus in the Gospels.* We might then correspond with that person, or people close to him, through the mail and carefully read the letters sent to us. *We have letters from those who walked with Jesus in Acts, the Epistles, and the book of Revelation.* But, of course, best of all would be taking the time to visit that person and spending time talking and listening carefully to what he had to say. *This is the opportunity we have in prayer, to talk with Him in our quiet places and get to know His heart by listening with our spiritual ears.*

However, if we come with preconceived notions and do all the talking ourselves, we know no more about that person when we leave than when we arrived. If we are truly going to know Jesus, then we must set aside our preconceived notions and come to Him ready to learn. We can judge against His Word what we hear during such times, for He will never contradict himself, and we can learn to know and discern His voice more clearly. As He said in John 10:

> He who enters by the door is a shepherd of the sheep. To him the doorkeeper opens, and the sheep hear his voice, and he calls his own sheep by name and leads them out. When he puts forth all his own, he goes ahead of them, and the sheep follow him *because they know his voice.* . . . I am the good shepherd. (John 10:2–4, 11 NASB)

Notice that the sheep have learned the Shepherd's voice because they have lived with Him habitually for some time. They do not just drop by once a week to spend an hour or so with Him. In fact, they make their way through life by following Him. They go where he leads and nowhere else. They don't choose a field and then try to get the Shepherd to come to them there; they go to the fields and streams where He leads them.

It is time for us to get real with God. Do we truly know Him or just know about Him? Sincere Christians can hamper what God is trying to do on the earth today because they are content to be "Christian" outwardly while continuing to follow their own desires inwardly.[6] The same thing that happened to the religious people in

> *It is time for us to get real with God. Do we truly know Him or just know about Him?*

the times of Jesus is what has happened today: We follow God through a prescribed list of do's and don'ts as opposed to a living relationship with a holy God.

Think about this for a moment and don't count yourself out too quickly. There was a time when I would have scoffed at the thought that I was living by a list of rules rather than following Christ personally . . . until I found out my actions were more dictated by trying to impress others with my "Christianity" than having the same priorities God has.

In the 1980s I was intoxicated by fleshly power with no idea how deceived I was. During the early days of the Reagan era, I was on the VIP list, invited time and again to the White House. Oh my, had I arrived! One day I would have lunch with the president of the United States or his cabinet, along with other religious leaders. A few months later I would be in a special briefing with Secretary of State Robert McFarland, boldly challenging him concerning the Word of God.

I was also once asked to briefly address the Republican National Convention when they met in Dallas, Texas, for a special session. Following the gathering, I was invited to a reception with the president's cabinet and some of the most powerful people in the world. Man, was I smoking! But the stink of my flesh hit me in the face one day as I was having lunch in the White House with the president and cabinet members and sitting next to Chuck Colson.

"Chuck," I asked, "have you been back since Watergate?"

"No," he replied, "this is my first time."

"You must be happy about these strategies, since you had a lot to do with them. After all, you were President Nixon's legal counsel."

"No, it's the last thing on my mind," he said. "I just felt the Lord wanted me to come, but what I'm really excited about is going to visit death row tonight to share the gospel."

Looking at Chuck Colson, I saw such brokenness and humility. He was anticipating his appointment with Jesus that night at the death house, not the White House. Yet many of us in that room were pushing and shoving, scheming and conniving to get our picture taken with the president and say a few words or slip a note to him. Christ surely was weeping. The only "who's who" list He cares about is whose name is written in the Lamb's Book of Life.

I was so polluted I was strutting like a rooster—arrogant, proud, hot-tempered, even offended when my wife did not treat me royally. *Doesn't she realize that I'm a man of God and a very, very important one at that?* What a stench in the nostrils of God!

What Is a Christian Without Christ?

We may be moral, support a conservative political agenda, and enroll our children in Christian schools yet still be a million miles from the heart of God. Our church may preach repentance like John the Baptist, with hundreds responding nightly, or we may be famous in Christian circles, yet we can be blind to Jesus Christ and drunk on our ambitions rather than sharing His heart for this world. We are obsessed with our slogans and pleased with the world's accolades. As the kingdoms we build (supposedly in His name) exhaust us, we promise Him that one day, when we have time, we'll get in hot pursuit of Him and Him alone.

If we don't realize that Jesus is still active in the earth today and wants so badly to touch His world through us, then it is because we don't truly know Him or His heart. If we are not touching lives around us with His power, it is because we do not understand His works and therefore cannot be a part of them.

If Jesus' prayer "that we would know God" has not come to pass, it is because we have not come into agreement with it by believing that knowing God personally is possible. We must pursue Him until we find Him. Only one thing affects our lives as significantly as Jesus' prayers and His sacrifice, and that is human will. Israel limited God's power through their unbelief in the desert,[7] so they wandered for forty years instead of going into the Promised Land. No matter how great Jesus' salvation is through the Cross, if a person rejects it, he will not be saved. If we are to live Jesus' ministry, we must first start by coming into agreement with this first prayer and seek to know God with all of our heart—for real!

What we don't know may not hurt us—but it definitely limits what God can do through us.

Jesus Has Called Us His Friends

The idea of friendship has become trivialized today because we take friendship so casually. If I asked what the difference between a friend and an acquaintance is, most of us would probably answer something like, "Well, a friend is someone I spend more time with because we enjoy doing the same things together. An acquaintance is simply someone I have only met a few times." Yet the Bible term for "friend" is grounded in covenant relationship. It expresses a bond and a mutual obligation of one person to another, as in marriage: "All I have—wealth, talent, time, and ability—is yours; and all you have—wealth, talent, time, and ability—is mine." With becoming friends in this sense, there is mutual obligation and dedication. True friendship is a bond that links destinies and resources together for present and future generations.

Most of us have sung the song "What a Friend We Have in Jesus," but is it possible that Jesus is also singing something like "What a friend I have in Mike Evans"? Sure, we can count on God to help us when we need Him, but is this a reciprocal relationship? Is the destiny of Jesus tied to our daily lives? Are we looking out for His interests even half as much as we expect Him to look out for ours? Certainly we have seen His power and goodness work on our behalf at some point in our Christian lives, but if we really want to see His power at work, shouldn't we be hooking up with what He is trying to accomplish on the earth today? Doesn't it seem logical that this is where the greater works will come in? Yet how are we ever going to better know what He wants to do on this earth if we aren't willing to draw close enough to Him to know His purposes?

On the same night Jesus prayed the prayer recorded in John 17, He said another incredible thing to His disciples:

> *This is my commandment, that ye love one another, as I have loved you.* Greater love hath no man than this, that a man lay down his life for his friends. *Ye are my friends,* if ye do whatsoever I command you. Henceforth I call you not servants; for the servant knoweth not what his lord doeth: but *I have called you friends*; for all things that I have heard of my Father I have made known unto you. Ye have not chosen me, but I have chosen you, and ordained you, that ye should go and bring forth fruit, and that your fruit should remain: that whatsoever ye shall ask of the Father in my name, he may give it you. These things I command you, that ye love one another. (John 15:12–17)

If I said that Jesus' greatest commandment was that we loved our neighbors as ourselves, I am sure some Christians would agree with a hearty "Amen, brother!" After all, when Jesus was asked what the great commandment was, that was His answer. But look at this passage again. Yes, it was Jesus' response to the question of what the great commandment was, but who was asking him? Old covenant believers who were under the law. Jesus' answer was that loving God with all your heart, soul, and mind and loving your neighbor as yourself were the great commandments—"On these two commandments hang all the law and the prophets."[8] I believe that for those of us under grace—no longer under the law and the prophets—His great commandment is in this passage: not that you "love your neighbor as yourself," but "that you love one another, *as Jesus has loved you.*"

Now, let me ask you, how can we possibly love a sick person *as Jesus loved that one* if we do not have the power available to us to see that person healed? Likewise, how can we love a mentally ill person, or someone possessed of a devil, if we don't have the supernatural knowledge to help them or to deliver them from the thing oppressing them? How can we possibly love a person in prison, someone on the street, someone who is poor and hungry, or someone who has just lost their home, with the same love Jesus loved if we don't have the power to multiply resources to help them as Jesus did with the little boy's lunch of fish and bread? How can Jesus honestly expect us to love the world as He did if we don't have the power to do the things He did? Obviously He didn't expect us to love like He did without His miracle-working power, because it was earlier that night that He also said, "He that believeth on me, the works that I do shall he do also; and greater works than these shall he do; because I go unto my Father."[9]

This is exactly what He meant again when He called us "His friends." He was in essence saying, "If you make all that you have available to Me for My purposes on the earth through your obedience, then I will make all that I have available to you to see those purposes fulfilled." He also said, "If you were just my servants, you wouldn't know what I am up to on the earth; but since you are my friends, I will reveal to you the will of My Father in everything and if you ask My Father anything in My Name, then He will give it to you. These things I have commanded *that you may love the world with the love with which I have loved you.*"

Paul described this New Testament relationship as well:

> God showed his great love for us by sending Christ to die for us while we were still sinners. And since we have been made right in God's sight by the blood of Christ, he will certainly save us from God's judgment. For since *we were restored to friendship with God by the death of his Son* while we were still his enemies, we will certainly be delivered from eternal punishment by his life. So now we can rejoice in our wonderful new relationship with God—*all because of what our Lord Jesus Christ has done for us in making us friends of God.* (Romans 5:8–11 NLT)

How well do you know this Jesus who has called you to be His friend?

During the Persian Gulf War, God sent me to Dhahran, Saudi Arabia. One morning as I prayed, Jesus softly said, "Son, I want you to go to the hotel. To the first man you see, I want you to extend your hand and say, 'May I go with you?' "

Obediently I went, and I shook the hand of a silk-gowned Arab whom I'd never met. Angrily he spat out, "Who are you?"

"May I go with you?" I asked.

"Who are you?" he said again.

"May I go with you?"

He griped at me, complained of being in a bad mood, then suddenly said, "Yes, be here at 6:15 tomorrow morning."

I left, having no idea who this man was or where we were going. The next day I was amazed when a dozen jeeps drove up, and in the fourth jeep sat a four-star general—Mohammed Kaleed—the man whose hand I had shook. When he saw my Bible he asked, "Are you a Christian?" I told him I was a minister.

"We behead ministers every Thursday," he stated flatly. "Would you like to go there with me too?"

"I'm busy Thursday," I said. He laughed.

"I like you," he replied with a smile.

Here I was loving a man who had just offered to behead me. Could it have been anything but the love of Christ?

He took me near the border of Kuwait to meet with the Syrian high command and the Egyptian Third Army, where they shared strategic invasion operations. He thought I had known what he was doing so he kept no secrets. I knew nothing, but Jesus knew everything. I was able to share the gospel with him and many other military personnel and soldiers on that trip. It was definitely a miraculous opportunity! But when I left, I thought that was all it was about.

Then, several years after that occasion, I preached in a crusade in the Philippines. A trio of Filipino pastors greeted me warmly after the meeting and even began to cry. I didn't think I'd preached well enough to put pastors to tears, so I asked them why they were weeping. Shocked that I didn't know, they told me they had been in jail in Dhahran—condemned to beheading for preaching the gospel. Then one day their jail cell doors flew open and Prince Mohammed Kaleed told them they could leave. They were weeping because they knew what I'd never known—they believed that my witness to Prince Mohammed Kaleed had saved their lives.

This is how Christ wants to live His life through us every day—this is what Jesus is praying for at the right hand of the Father. He wants us to know God's will and walk in it every day. He longs for unbroken fellowship on His terms so He can reveal to the world the fullness of His glory. He is able to do "exceeding abundantly above all that we ask or think"[10] if we will only come into agreement with His unanswered prayers.

Are We All That We Can Be?

I believe in these last days that there will be a new moving within the body of Christ, where people no longer follow another person, a denomination, a revival, or a movement, or anything man originates, but they will link up with God individually to walk as an army, receiving their orders directly from Him. In this way they will be molded together to do His works and preach His Word and not be caught up with ego and self-sufficiency or concerned with who gets the glory or the financial reward. Their desire will be like that of Jesus: "to do the will of Him that sent me, and to finish His work."[11]

Jesus longs to be known today.

Jesus longs to be known today. Those who know Him should carry a sense of destiny about them. This is sadly untrue of most Christians today. We have no sense of destiny, little sense of purpose, and are indistinguishable in a crowd from those who seek little else but their own selfish desires. When was the last time someone hungry for God walked up to you and said, "There is something about you . . . I can't place it! You have such peace. You seem so happy. What is your secret?" How often have you had such an opportunity to share about your Lord and Savior?

Those who know Jesus and spend real time with Him have such things happen to them. I have had people I once shook hands with bang on my door in the middle of the night, asking me to tell them about the God they are seeking. I have had people drop to their knees before other ministers and myself, acknowledging their sin before us and asking how they might receive God's forgiveness. When you meet people who have been with Jesus, you are instantly humbled. You see Jesus in their eyes. You know that they know Him!

Why don't all of us know Jesus in this way?

CHAPTER THREE

The Weakest Link

That they may be one: as thou, Father, art in me, and I also in thee, that they also may be one in us.

JOHN 17:21

I was in Wales at an international ministers' conference when I read the passage, "Of the angels he saith, 'Who maketh his angels spirits, and his ministers a flame of fire,' "[1] just before I was to get up to speak.

Immediately Jesus spoke softly to me, "Ask them, 'Are you one?' and sit down."

I wondered at this for only a moment, but when I was called up, I simply did what Jesus had told me to do. I walked up to the podium, asked, "Are you one?" and then returned to my seat.

Never have I seen such glory fall, as the power of God hit that place without anyone saying another word. The anointing took over the meeting to such a degree that at one o'clock the following morning, executives of the denomination were still caught up in glory. The certificates for those who were to be ordained that night were laid on their chests as they lay on the ground like dead men. They could not stand in the presence of a holy God.

After this I had a new revelation of the importance God puts on unity in His body.

Division in the Ranks of God's Army

The second unanswered prayer that Jesus prayed in John 17 is "That they may be one as we are one,"[2] or, in other words, that we would be one with each other in the same way that Jesus and His Father are one. That is a pretty close bond.

Yet according to the latest edition of the *World Christian Encyclopedia,* there are now nearly thirty-four thousand denominations and para-denominations that call themselves Christian.[3] How can we have one God, one Bible, and one body of Christ and yet have so many walls built between us?

The answer is relatively simple: Self is on the throne. The weakest link in the universal body of Christ is not between church and church or brother and brother but *between each of us individually and Jesus himself.* It is between what we want to do for God and what God is actually trying to do through each of us. In our own flesh and pride, we have built kingdoms in His name but for our own purposes. Or we have taken sincere moves of God under true men and women of God and turned them into organizations that eventually have little or nothing to do with what God was originally doing through their "founders." This is a struggle that has gone on in the church since the first split. We separate from one another by majoring in the minor doctrines and in our own desires instead of concentrating on being like Jesus.

> *We separate from one another by majoring in the minor doctrines and in our own desires instead of concentrating on being like Jesus.*

Who Is on the Throne of Your Life?

In the 1960s there emerged a little pamphlet called *The Four Spiritual Laws.* You may have seen it.[4] One of the most remarkable things I remember about it is the little circle diagram that was used to represent the world of an individual and his interests. It has always struck me as a clear illustration of what happens in our lives with or without Jesus.

At the center of the circle was a little chair that represented who or what ruled the life of the individual. The little booklet called it "the throne of your life." Whoever sat in it directed all the events of that person's life. The circle representing self on the throne had an "S" on the chair and showed all the little circles or dots representing the things in one's life going every which way and running into one another in chaos. The circle showing Jesus on the throne of our lives had a cross on the chair with all of the little circles or dots with orderly, straight lines directing each of them smoothly out from the center like the rays going out from a sun in a child's drawing.

The booklet said we have a choice: We can either put self on the throne of our life and suffer from the chaos that follows, or we can put Christ on the throne of our life and let His wisdom and guidance direct our paths. That choice is made day by day and minute by minute. This pamphlet was designed to bring non-believers to Christ.

Paul, however, addressed the same issue to the Christians in Corinth. Here were Spirit-filled believers who walked as if they were unsaved—following their fleshly desires and causing divisions and strife in the Corinthian church.[5] Despite having confessed Jesus as their Lord, they chose to keep their selves on the throne. Because of this, despite the fact that the testimony of Christ was confirmed in them and that they hadn't fallen behind in the gifts of the Spirit,[6] their effectiveness in transforming their community was extremely limited.

The Galatians had a similar problem, only they weren't giving in to their fleshly desires but rather trying to perfect themselves in Christ by turning back to the traditions and laws of Judaism, from which Christ had freed them. They were choosing to walk by the flesh in setting up rules and laws to control themselves instead of following the leadership of His Spirit. Paul cautioned them:

You foolish Galatians, who has bewitched you, before whose eyes Jesus Christ was publicly portrayed as crucified? This is the only thing I want to find out from you: did you receive the Spirit by the works of the Law, or by hearing with faith? Are you so foolish? Having begun by the Spirit, are you now being perfected by the flesh? . . . So then, does He who provides you with the Spirit and works miracles among you, do it by the works of the Law, or by hearing with faith? (Galatians 3:1–3, 5 NASB)

Paul had a similar word for the Colossians:

If you have died with Christ to the elementary principles of the world, why, as if you were living in the world, do you submit yourself to decrees, such as, "Do not handle, do not taste, do not touch!" (which all refer to things destined to perish with use)—in accordance with the commandments and teachings of men? These are matters which have, to be sure, the appearance of wisdom in self-made religion and self-abasement and severe treatment of the body, but are of no value against fleshly indulgence. (Colossians 2:20–23 NASB)

In other words, "If you have been born again through the Holy Spirit of God, why is it that you are trying to live in God's righteousness through the rules and dry religion of men and denominations rather than living by the law of love and following the leadership of the Holy Spirit? No wonder you no longer walk in God's miracle power: You have forsaken His present-day ministry either for your own fleshy desires or to build your own kingdoms—your own 'ministries'—using His name! No wonder you can't even get along with each other!"

Don't get me wrong, there *are* some doctrines that separate Christian groups from non-Christian groups; there *are* basic tenets of the Christian faith that are evident in the Bible. We cannot forsake these and still be Christians. But, as a whole, those who call themselves Christians and divide themselves into various denominations from others who also call Jesus Lord aren't so much wrong about the basic tenets of faith—they simply don't know God in all of His divine power and glory. Those who don't know something will often come to wrong conclusions—this is only natural. Most of our reasons for division and strife would begin to disappear if we simply spent ten minutes in the presence of Jesus and understood what it truly meant to put Him on the throne of our lives.

These are the two extremes of putting self on the throne: (1) Living by selfish or fleshly desires; or (2) Living by "religious" rules, created by men, to define holiness. Though option #2 seems much more acceptable, it is just as much a form of self worship as option #1, and just as debilitating to what God would like to do on the earth today, if not more so, because such people think they know God, while they are actually about a million miles away from *truly* knowing Him. Where self rules, there is little or no room for the works of the Holy Spirit and God's miracle-working power. We have to make the choice: Will we live by the flesh (self) or the Spirit?[7]

Life in the Spirit is the only path toward oneness with God.

The Lord Our God Is One Lord With One Body

The oneness of God is a key theme throughout the Old Testament. *Sh'ma Yisrael Adonai Elohaynu Adonai Echad*—"Hear, O Israel, the Lord our God is One." Jesus even echoes this when asked about the great, or first, commandment:

> And one of the scribes came, and . . . asked him, "Which is the first commandment of all?" And Jesus answered him, "The first of all the commandments is, *Hear, O Israel; The Lord our God is one Lord*: And thou shalt love the Lord thy God with all thy heart, and with all thy soul, and with all thy mind, and with all thy strength: this is the first commandment" (Mark 12:28–30).

How could God's oneness breed various sects or groups to follow Him? Paul expressed concern about this same question in Ephesians:

With all lowliness and meekness, with longsuffering, forbearing one another in love; Endeavoring to *keep the unity of the Spirit in the bond of peace.* There is one body, and one Spirit, even as ye are called in one hope of your calling; One Lord, one faith, one baptism, One God and Father of all, who is above all, and through all, and in you all. (Ephesians 4:2–6)

Another way of saying this might be, "If all of these things are one—One God and Father of all, one Lord, one faith, one baptism, one Spirit, and so on—then there is also only one body that will be following Him. If we forbear one another in love and walk in humility, then this unity will be preserved in a bond of peace." Paul must have seen that even though the church was only one organization at this time, division and strife within that body were already a real threat to the work God had for them to do.

He echoed this to the Philippians:

If there be therefore any consolation in Christ, if any comfort of love, if any fellowship of the Spirit, if any bowels and mercies, Fulfill ye my joy, that ye *be likeminded, having the same love, being of one accord, of one mind.* Let nothing be done through strife or vainglory; but in lowliness of mind *let each esteem other better than themselves.* (Philippians 2:1–3)

Paul must also have been well acquainted with the divisions that occurred among the Jews. The "body of believers" Jesus came to was already divided into several sects before He was even born. The Jewish leaders had sectioned themselves into groups with different interpretations of the Scriptures: Pharisees, Sadducees, scribes, etc.

Did Jesus even single out one of these groups and say anything like "Now, you Sadducees, let me show you where the Pharisees have it right and you have missed it"? No, He simply lumped them all together as people who needed God and whose traditions had made His Word ineffective in their lives.

> Why do ye also transgress the commandment of God by your tradition? . . . Ye made the commandment of God of none effect by your tradition. Ye hypocrites, well did [Isaiah] prophesy of you, saying, This people draweth nigh unto me with their mouth, and honoreth me with their lips; but their heart is far from me. But in vain they do worship me, teaching for doctrines the commandments of men. (Matthew 15:3, 6–9)

Jesus didn't care what group they belonged to—in fact, we see cases where He didn't even care if they were Jewish or not![8] Jesus only cared about one thing in this regard: that each person He encountered knew he or she had direct access to God His Father *individually*. He came to remove the things that kept the people from God so that they could easily come to make the choice to follow God wholeheartedly for themselves. What was it they needed? Healing? Revelation of the truth? Provision? Freedom? Jesus became an instant link between people's needs and God wherever He went in His ministry.

Nowhere do we hear Him saying, "No, I can't do that for you. God wants you to suffer through this for a while to teach you something." No, He never refused a sincere heart seeking after God. What we do see, however, is His asking hard questions of those who came to Him with fleshly motives—whether they were selfish or religious—and those people turning away on their own because they weren't willing to let go of their own selfishness to follow Him with pure hearts. His purpose was always to help in bringing people to the knowledge of the gospel.

The prophet Zephaniah foretold of a people God would rescue, people who live in this kind of purpose:

> For then will I turn to the people a pure language, that they may all call upon the name of the LORD, to serve him *with one consent*. (Zephaniah 3:9)

The Hebrew here for "with one consent" is *shâkem echad*, which means literally "with one shoulder." To me, this brings up the image of several people together trying to move a large boulder by putting their shoulders together as one to push it out of the way. This is God's model for how His church should operate—all of us together putting our shoulders to the things that keep others from seeing God clearly and heaving these obstacles out of the way through our unified effort. This may sound difficult, until we realize that the biggest shoulder right there next to ours is Jesus' own. The problem is that most of us never put our shoulder to the boulder with Him because we are too caught up in other things. We haven't come into agreement with His prayers.

> Two are better than one; because they have a good reward for their labor. For if they fall, the one will lift up his fellow: but woe to him that is alone when he falleth; for he hath not another to help him up. Again, if two lie together, then they have heat: but how can one be warm alone? And if one prevail against him, two shall withstand him; and a threefold cord is not quickly broken. (Ecclesiastes 4:9–12)

When we know God and walk as one with Him and His purposes, we are never alone. When we come into agreement with Him and His Word, binding ourselves together with them as if we were three strands of the same rope—"a threefold cord is not easily broken"—then the most amazing things can happen! All we need are hearts hungry enough to believe His Word and act upon it in His wisdom.

While I was still in Bible school, I was sitting with a friend in the cafeteria reading my Bible as rain poured down outside. For the first time I came across the passage "He was wounded for our transgressions, he was bruised for our iniquities, the chastisement of our peace was upon Him; and with His stripes we are healed" (Isaiah 53:5). Another friend, Billy D'Angelo, walked in right at that moment. A victim of multiple sclerosis, he wore hip-high leg braces and had holes in the knees of his pants from falling down, because even special shoes and braces would not hold his legs steady all the time.

"Billy, you were healed," I said, showing him the verse.

"I've been in church all my life, and I haven't been healed yet," he said.

The glory of God was so strong it felt like a thousand volts of electricity.

Another friend, Randy Van Pay, and I brought Billy into a prayer room where we prayed for two hours, just three young men on our faces before God. Suddenly a white cloud descended from the ceiling down the walls to where we were on the floor.

The glory of God was so strong it felt like a thousand volts of electricity. If you moved your hand, the air felt thick. As the cloud touched Billy, his legs straightened. He threw off the braces, ran outside into a muddy field, and stood weeping. Seeing his braces gone, students started running toward him but spun and fell into the mud under the power of the Holy Spirit. It was an incredible move of God!

Several years later I spoke at a crusade in Uganda. When I took the platform, I simply held up my Bible and said, "The Word of God is the power of God unto salvation." People by the thousands in that meeting—many of them Muslims—started shaking as if they were plugged into a 220-volt outlet. As I held up the Word, they took off demonic fetishes from around their waists and wrists and threw them into piles, then burned the piles, denouncing the powers of darkness. Something happened in the heavenlies, in the spirit realm, that brought this incredible break-through. The anointing was on Christ and His Word! It was astonishing.

The True Purpose of the Church

In the entire Gospels, Jesus only taught His disciples one prayer. Today we call it the Lord's Prayer. Though many of us recite it from memory in services or on occasions where various denominations gather together, how often do we really think about it or expect this prayer to be answered? Look at it again a moment and think about praying it as if you were binding your-self together with the words of the prayer and God to see these requests accomplished on the earth:

> Our Father which art in heaven,
> Hallowed be thy name.
> Thy kingdom come.
> Thy will be done in earth,
> as it is in heaven.
> Give us this day our daily bread.
> And forgive us our debts,
> as we forgive our debtors.
> And lead us not into temptation,
> but deliver us from evil:
> For thine is the kingdom,
> and the power, and the glory,
> for ever. Amen. (Matthew 6:9–13)

This simple and profound prayer says,

(1) I worship and praise you;
(2) I want your kingdom to be realized on earth just as it is in heaven;
(3) I will trust in your provision;
(4) I will forgive others as you have forgiven me;
(5) Through your strength I will resist temptation and avoid evil;
(6) Because you are the owner of the kingdom, power, and glory that will last forever;
(7) Amen (which means, "so let it be").[9]

To me, everything wrapped up in being a Christian is con-tained in this prayer, and the main purpose for being a Christian is right there at the beginning: "Thy kingdom come. Thy will be done in earth, as it is in heaven."

The true purpose of the church—the body of Christ on the earth today—is simply to see His will done here as it is in heaven.

The Kingdom of Heaven

Look for a moment at what Jesus said the kingdom of heaven is like:

(1) A grain of mustard seed—it may start as the smallest of all things, but when it is planted and grows, it becomes a place of shelter, lodging, and protection.[10]

(2) Yeast—though it is only added to a small part of something, it will soon permeate and change everything it comes into contact with.[11]

(3) A hidden treasure and a pearl of great price—for the joy of having this one thing, a person would be willing to sell everything else he owns to possess it,[12] and those who trust in their wealth and possessions rather than in God will have a hard time entering into it.[13]

(4) A net—which when it is cast into the sea will return full to the boat with every kind of fish.[14]

(5) A man hiring workers for his vineyard and a king inviting guests to his son's wedding—those who come to it will receive its reward whether they come early or late, and though many are invited, only those who answer the call will enjoy its benefits: "For many are called, but few are chosen."[15]

The true purpose of the church—the body of Christ on the earth today—is simply to see His will done here as it is in heaven.

Jesus told us that we should pray that this comes about on earth as it does in heaven. This is what the church was left on earth to do: usher in His kingdom. How can we possibly do this if we truly do not know Him and are not one with Him?

Jesus gave a simple illustration of this to His disciples. I think most of us tend to miss a nuance of this teaching that would help to clarify what I am talking about. Please carefully read the following passage:

At the same time came the disciples unto Jesus, saying,

"Who is the greatest in the kingdom of heaven?"

And Jesus called a little child unto him, and set him in the midst of them, And said, "Verily I say unto you, Except ye be converted, and *become as little children,* ye shall not enter into the kingdom of heaven. Whosoever therefore shall humble himself *as this little child,* the same is greatest in the kingdom of heaven" (Matthew 18:1–4).

Most of us have heard this story before, or even heard a sermon or two on it, and come away with the message that we should be like little children before God if we want to enter His kingdom. We have centered on the point that we should have the attributes of children—innocence, trustfulness, simplicity—as the central meaning of this passage. And this certainly is an important part of it, but *it is not the answer to the disciples' question.* Look at the passage again, and you will see Jesus' response is twofold: (1) Except you become as *a* little child, you shall not enter the kingdom of heaven, and (2) whoever shall humble himself as *this* little child shall become the greatest in the kingdom of heaven.

Jesus is being very specific here in this second point: It is not the general principle of childlikeness alone that ushers us into living God's kingdom on earth today, but there is something special about *this one child* that will teach us great things about living in God's kingdom. Was it who the child was? Was he some saint that would do great things later in life? Was Jesus showing the disciples someone they should look to for guidance later after He was gone?

The passage gives us no suggestion of this. In fact, the key to what Jesus was teaching is plainly in what He said: "Whosoever therefore shall humble himself as (or like) this little child . . ." The point was not in who the child was but *in what the child did.* How did he humble himself? *He simply did what Jesus asked without hesitation and without question.*

Picture the scene again: The disciples ask Jesus a question, and in response Jesus turns around and sees a little boy walking by, perhaps carrying water for his parents or on some other task, or maybe simply running down the street, playing with his friends.

Jesus says, "Child," catching the boy's attention, "come here." The boy stopped whatever else he was doing, however important his errand or however much he may have been enjoying his play, and walked over to Jesus in obedience. He didn't say, "Sure, Jesus, just as soon as I finish what I am doing." Nor did he say, "Aw, can't I finish my game first?" No, he went immediately, without saying a word. Then Jesus takes the boy lovingly by the shoulders and, facing him to the disciples, says, "Whosoever shall humble himself *as* this little child, the same is greatest in the kingdom of heaven."

> *I had no idea that my desperate heart's cry was the fertile soil in which the glory of God could be manifested.*

This is what I have experienced again and again in my life, though more often by accident than intent. At times when I was completely dependent upon God, knowing I could do nothing in my own strength, stripped of all self-confidence, my desperate prayer would be, "God, if you don't do it, it can't be done." Then I simply did what God told me to do in response. I had no idea that my desperate heart's cry was the fertile soil in which the glory of God could be manifested. Now I see clearly that those times when Jesus has moved most powerfully were when I leaned the most heavily upon Him. When He has moved most powerfully was when "I" moved out. Jesus would show up and softly speak, and when I obeyed, I would see His will done on the earth as if we were actually standing before His throne in heaven. This is receiving the kingdom of God like a child.

> Suffer the little children to *come unto me,* and forbid them not: *for of such is the kingdom of God.* Verily I say unto you, Whosoever shall not receive the kingdom of God as a little child, he shall not enter therein. (Mark 10:14–15)

It is through those that have spent time with Jesus—and obey His voice—that His kingdom becomes real on the earth.

Many Parts; One Purpose

Please don't misunderstand what I am saying here: I am not calling for some huge ecumenical movement among all those that call themselves Christians to all join back together into one universal, corporate church organization. I don't care any more than Jesus did if you want to call yourself a Baptist, a Methodist, a Presbyterian, a Charismatic, or a Slice-and-Dice-O-Matic, for that matter—I only want to know: Do you *know* Jesus? Have you been with Him? Are you taking part in *His* plans to bring to fruition His kingdom on the earth? Are you obeying His unique plan for your life? *Are you one with Him?*

If all of us would just be one with Jesus, we would have no problem working together in the earth to bring forth His kingdom, no matter what we want to call ourselves or what our function is in His plan. This is why His church is compared to a body with many parts that all have different functions but work together, building up the body in unity of purpose and the love of God. Look at how Paul described it in Ephesians:

Therefore it says,

"When He ascended on high,
He led captive a host of captives,
And He gave gifts to men."

. . . for the equipping of the saints for the work of service, to the building up of the body of Christ; *until we all attain to the unity of the faith, and of the knowledge of the Son of God,* to a mature man, to the measure of the stature which belongs to the fullness of Christ.

As a result, we are no longer to be children, tossed here and there by waves and carried about by every wind of doctrine, by the trickery of men, by craftiness in deceitful scheming; but *speaking the truth in love, we are to grow up in all aspects into Him who is the head, even Christ, from whom the whole body, being fitted and held together by what every joint supplies, according to the proper working of each individual part, causes the growth of the body for the building up of itself in love.* (Ephesians 4:8, 12–16 NASB)

David wrote of it in this way:

Behold, how good and how pleasant it is for brethren to dwell together in unity! It is like the precious ointment upon the head, that ran down upon the beard, even Aaron's beard: that went down to the skirts of his garments; As the dew of Hermon, and as the dew that descended upon the mountains of Zion: for there the LORD commanded the blessing, even life for evermore. (Psalm 133)

According to *Vine's,* the word "together" here "emphasizes a plurality in unity. In some contexts the connotation is on community in action."[16] David is saying that the place where brothers and sisters work together in this kind of unity is the place of God's anointing! It is a place where we are refreshed and strengthened by God's Spirit as the dew nourishes the grass! It is the place where God *commands* blessing! And it is the place where *zoe*— the eternal, God-kind-of-life—flows freely!

Only when self is subjugated to Christ will we be one with God—and each other—to have this kind of unity. We will never be one by trying to agree with one another and putting aside differences of belief for the sake of unity alone. We are to be one as Jesus and His Father are one. Only when Jesus is on the throne in each of our lives individually can we be in tune with His purpose and be one body on earth, able to work corporately to bring true and lasting revival. Only when self is subjugated to Jesus will His "greater works" flourish as the body of Christ grows up into His fullness and carries forth His kingdom on the earth.

This is what atonement—"at-one-ment"—is all about: *We must be one with Jesus.*

CHAPTER FOUR

Living With Jesus' Joy

That they might have my joy fulfilled in themselves.

JOHN 17:13

It must have seemed dark days for all of them. The city around them lay in ruins. Even as they struggled to rebuild and repair it, they carried with them the constant fear that they would be assaulted again. They worked with mortar, trowel, and brick in one hand, and a spear or sword in the other to defend themselves if the need arose. Stone by stone they rebuilt the wall, watched the hills surrounding them for any sign of attack, and only ventured once in a while to let their vigilance drift to thoughts of the day when the city walls would be fully repaired, when they could leave this labor for the work of rebuilding the temple. They hoped in their God, a God they knew remotely, and longed for His presence to once more dwell in the midst of their city.

When the walls were finally completed, the people gathered on the first day of the seventh month, the beginning of the Feast of Trumpets, and the priest mounted a platform to address the crowds. There he opened the book, and at this the people stood. From early morning until midday he read from it the law they had been given through Moses. In response to hearing the word of their Lord that had been so far from them in the time of their exile, the people shouted praises and called out "Amen! Amen!— So be it! So be it!" and wept under the conviction that in recent years they had so freely violated God's laws without even knowing it. Many fell to their faces on the ground and cried out for forgiveness from God, their tears mixing with the dust.

At the sight of their lamentations, their leader, Nehemiah, rose before them and called out:

> "Don't weep on such a day as this! For today is a sacred day before the LORD your God. . . . Go and celebrate with a feast of choice foods and sweet drinks, and share gifts of food with people who have nothing prepared. This is a sacred day before our Lord. Don't be dejected and sad, *for the joy of the LORD is your strength!*" (Nehemiah 8:9–10 NLT).

The Scriptures also record the people's response to this:

> So the people went away to eat and drink at a festive meal, to share gifts of food, and to celebrate with great joy *because they had heard God's words and understood them.* (Nehemiah 8:12 NLT)

The next day they rose up and began to do what they had heard and understood from God's Word, making sure all in the region who didn't know of it knew and understood His law so they could each walk in it and keep His ways.[1]

I am sure that many have heard Nehemiah 8:10 before— "The joy of the Lord is your strength"—but how many of us are familiar with the story behind it? In the midst of a people defeated, fearful, and trying to rebuild their nation and their faith came a return to the Word of God. This renewal brought tears of conviction and guilt from those who knew they had been ignorant of the truth of God's Word all their lives, though they had also called upon His name and reverenced it all of their days. It was into this atmosphere that Nehemiah spoke these often-repeated words.

Are we in America—who are trying to rebuild our faith and

our defenses in the face of terrorism, recession, corporate scandals that rock the stock market, etc.—that much different from those trying to rebuild Jerusalem in the days of Nehemiah? If you are a person who has picked up this book and feels convicted because you have now seen from the Scriptures that it is time to truly get to know God and be one with His purposes, then my word to you is the same as Nehemiah's was to the people of God in his time: "Stop your crying and rejoice! It is time to see His Word accomplished! The joy of the Lord Jesus is your strength!"

The Joy of *Your* Lord

In John 17, Jesus' third unanswered prayer was "That they might have my joy fulfilled in themselves."[2] Imagine that: Living in the same joy Jesus lived in on the earth! This is an amazing prayer and an amazing challenge to the body of Christ. Would anyone looking at the church today as a whole really call us joyful? Would they even call us a happy people, overall? The fact is that our churches are filled with discouraged people looking for fulfillment just as I was that day in my professor's office. We are God's frozen chosen—His own pickled people—sitting in our pews and daring our ministers to get us to smile. Is that the body that has been called to live in Jesus' joy?

It is, but it is not the body living in His joy. Where have we missed it?

Before we can answer this we must first understand exactly what Jesus' joy was. A quick word search of the Scriptures will show some interesting aspects of joy. In the Old Testament, we see joy expressed by the people of Israel when they had been victorious in battle, when David brought the ark of the covenant back to Jerusalem, when Solomon was crowned king to succeed his father, and when the temple was finally rebuilt and rededicated in

> *We are God's frozen chosen—His own pickled people—sitting in our pews and daring our ministers to get us to smile.*

the time of Ezra and Nehemiah. When Israel was delivered from Babylonian captivity, the psalmist expressed it this way:

> When the LORD turned again the captivity of Zion, we were like them that dream. Then was our mouth filled with laughter, and our tongue with singing: then said they among the heathen, "The LORD hath done great things for them." The LORD hath done great things for us; whereof we are glad.
>
> Turn again our captivity, O LORD, as the streams in the south. They that sow in tears shall reap in joy. He that goeth forth and weepeth, bearing precious seed, shall doubtless come again with rejoicing, bringing his sheaves with him. (Psalm 126)

The book of Proverbs also tells us,

> The desire accomplished is sweet to the soul. (Proverbs 13:19)

In the New Testament, Jesus gives this example of what joy is when He is preparing His disciples for His crucifixion and resurrection:

> Verily, verily, I say unto you, that ye shall weep and lament, but the world shall rejoice: and ye shall be sorrowful, but your sorrow shall be turned into joy. *A woman when she is in travail hath sorrow, because her hour is come: but as soon as she is delivered of the child, she remembereth no more the anguish, for joy that a man is born into the world.* And ye now therefore have sorrow: but I will see you again, and your heart shall rejoice, and your joy no man taketh from you. (John 16:20–22)

John the Baptist gave this example:

> They came to John and said to him, "Rabbi, that man who was with you on the other side of the Jordan—the one you testified about—well, he is baptizing, and everyone is going to him."

To this John replied, "A man can receive only what is given him from heaven. You yourselves can testify that I said, 'I am not the Christ but am sent ahead of him.' The bride belongs to the bridegroom. *The friend who attends the bridegroom waits and listens for him, and is full of joy when he hears the bridegroom's voice. That joy is mine, and it is now complete.* He must become greater; I must become less" (John 3:26–30 NIV).

Elsewhere in the Gospels, we see joy expressed at the birth and resurrection of Jesus and at the returning of the seventy to Jesus after He had sent them out to "Heal the sick, cleanse the lepers, raise the dead, cast out devils."[3] In the book of Acts we also see joy when many were healed in Samaria, when Peter was delivered by the angel from prison in answer to the prayers of the early believers, and at various times during the missionary trips of Paul when believers heard that others had received the Word of God and accepted Jesus.

If you look closely at these examples you will discover some interesting things about joy:

(1) Joy comes after victory—and victory does not come without a battle or a struggle (as in war or the birth of a child).

(2) People turn from tears to joy—joy often comes after a period of sorrow or loss (as at the time of an exile coming to an end). According to *Vine's*: "Experiences of sorrow prepare for, and enlarge, the capacity for 'joy.' "[4]

(3) Joy comes when something desired for so long is finally manifest (as the fulfillment of prophecy—such as the coming of the Messiah).

(4) Joy always seems to come in connection with the will of God being done (as at the receiving of the Word of God by others after persecutions or when Israel was delivered from her seventy years of exile).

Joy can thus be contrasted with "happiness" (a state in which we are blessed, often in unexpected ways) or "contentment" (where we choose to be satisfied with our present state for that which we have already). *Joy always seems to come when something that was hoped for has been realized after we have struggled and endured to receive it or as the result of struggling or enduring to receive something promised.* Joy is something that is won!

Look at another example Jesus gave in the parable of the talents (Matthew 25:14–30):

> And so he that had received five talents came and brought other five talents, saying, "Lord, thou deliveredst unto me five talents: behold, I have gained beside them five talents more." His lord said unto him, "Well done, thou good and faithful servant: thou hast been faithful over a few things, I will make thee ruler over many things: *enter thou into the joy of thy lord.*" He also that had received two talents came and said, "Lord, thou deliveredst unto me two talents: behold, I have gained two other talents beside them." His lord said unto him, "Well done, good and faithful servant; thou hast been faithful over a few things, I will make thee ruler over many things: *enter thou into the joy of thy lord*" (Matthew 25:20–23).

In this parable, Jesus likens the kingdom of God to a man who has gone away and left tasks for His servants. Those who entered into "the joy of their lord" were those who used what He gave them to increase His kingdom, and those who were reproved were those who did nothing with what they were given. *Entering into His joy thus comes from fulfilling His tasks on the earth with what He has given us!*

This was Jesus' joy—fulfilling the will of His Father. The Bible tells us in the book of Hebrews: "Jesus . . . *for the joy that was set before him* endured the cross, despising the shame" (Hebrews 12:2).

What was the joy that was set before Him? *The manifestation of God's kingdom on the earth in the life of everyone who believed on Him.*

When do we see Jesus the most joyful and satisfied in the Gospels?

(1) After He had spoken to the woman at Jacob's well in Samaria (John 4): "I have meat to eat that ye know not of. . . . My meat is to do the will of him that sent me, and to finish his work" (John 4:32, 34).

(2) When others showed unprecedented faith (the Roman centurion or the Syrophenician woman): "When Jesus heard it, *he marvelled,* and said to them that followed, 'Verily I say unto you, I have not found so great faith, no, not in Israel' " (Matthew 8:10).

(3) When the seventy returned to Him, having walked in His miraculous power: "And the seventy returned again with joy, saying, 'Lord, even the devils are subject unto us through thy name.' . . . In that hour Jesus rejoiced in spirit" (Luke 10:17, 21).

All of these were cases where the will of God was manifested on the earth. Jesus' joy was (and is) when His Father's will was done on earth as in heaven.

Joy Is Won . . .

So before Jesus could know this joy in seeing God's will manifested on the earth, He had to

(1) know God's will;
(2) align himself with that will; and
(3) do what God had instructed Him to do through the Holy Spirit to make that will a reality.

The rest was up to God. Jesus was not concerned with whether God's will was to be manifested immediately or gradually; He only made sure He did and said those things His Father had directed Him to do and say.[5]

Thus, for us as well, joy comes from knowing the will of God, aligning ourselves with it through prayer and agreement with His Word, and acting according to the leadership of His Holy Spirit. Until we truly know God, get a sense of His purpose and mission for our lives, plug into it, and start to walk in it, we will not know the same joy that Jesus did. While we may be happy, blessed, and content, we will never experience His joy except in the fulfillment of God's purposes for our lives or in the lives of those around us. *Real joy is grounded in the fulfillment of the will of God. It comes from knowing and fulfilling the Word and will of God!*

But Joy Can Also Be Taken by Faith

> *While we may be happy, blessed, and content, we will never experience His joy except in the fulfillment of God's purposes for our lives or in the lives of those around us.*

Many of us have probably experienced at least a bit of His joy when we saw a friend saved—or when we were saved ourselves—or when we experienced the will of God being manifest for ourselves or someone we know. But as New Testament believers, we don't have to wait for something to happen to have joy! *We can have joy when we realize that God has promised something to us, because if He has said it, then we have the assurance that it will happen.*

If we have God's Word on something, then we can rejoice. We can rejoice in our hope of heaven, we can rejoice that Jesus will come again, and we can rejoice that the kingdom of darkness is eternally defeated. Why? Because, like the simple song says, "the Bible tells me so."

Therefore, by faith we can look at any circumstance, see what God has promised about it, and rejoice! If we know God's will and are walking in His purposes, then we have a great deal of room for His joy, regardless of how things appear—for "faith is the substance of things hoped for, the evidence of things not seen."[6]

It was an extremely hot summer in Canada, where I was preaching at a camp meeting. My birthday happened to fall during it, June 30, so I took a morning off and my friend Bill

Fletcher and I went fishing. We found a boat on a lake, with a guide named Harry, who took us out. To use a biblical phrase, "We fished and caught nothing." Bill had been asleep for almost an hour when I finally laid down, praying and complaining over the time and money wasted. To make matters worse, I had to listen to Harry, who seemingly every five minutes was cursing the name of my Lord and Savior. While I grumbled, Jesus softly said, "I sent you here because I am going to catch a fish."

I turned my head and looked at Harry and realized what Jesus was saying. I asked the Lord to forgive my whining, sat up, and started sharing the gospel with Harry. As I did, Bill woke up and started praying softly. Little did I know what was about to take place.

"Harry," I said, "you see that pole there with the line in the water—there's a hook on it with bait. Now, Harry, if a big fish got on that hook and the line started going out and you started screaming, 'Set the hook!' and I did nothing, then I would never have the joy of catching that big fish. Harry, you are that big fish that Jesus wants to catch today."

As I said that, the line went screeching. Harry's face turned white. "I can't believe it," he said. "This has to be God."

"Set the hook!" he screamed. "Set the hook!"

What a joy it was for me to pull in an enormous trout (14 lbs. 11 oz.) on my birthday. Harry was astonished. He shouted repeatedly, "I can't believe it! It's the biggest rainbow trout I have ever seen in my life!"

Then he said, "Pray for me; I want to receive Jesus."

I prayed for Harry and noticed the precious tears filling his eyes as he experienced the living Christ. As we arrived back at the dock, his fishing buddies, whose boats had already come in, asked, "Harry, did you catch anything?"

"Oh!" he said, "two huge fish were caught today. That preacher caught the biggest rainbow I've ever seen, and Jesus caught me."

Walking in His Shadow

When we live our lives spending time with God to get to know Him and His purposes, opening our "self" to consider and be part of manifesting His kingdom on the earth, we should have a constant joy welling up and spilling out from within us. It should be an infectious joy that others want to be a part of. It should be the same thing that was in Jesus, and it should attract people to us as it did to Him. People should know we are different because of our joy. If we are truly walking with Jesus, letting Him guide our steps, then we should be constantly experiencing the benefits of His Spirit. Just as those who were healed when Peter's shadow fell over them, we should be more fully experiencing the benefits of the Holy Spirit as we follow closely behind Jesus.

But again, here is that struggle between self and putting on Christ, between the flesh and the spirit; really it is the struggle between our discontent and walking in Jesus' joy! This is why our churches are known more for hypocrisy than for joy: we are walking in our flesh rather than His Spirit.

Redefining "Self"

To this point, I have equated "self" with what the Bible calls "flesh": The part of us tied to the sin nature we had before coming to Christ, and the part of us that lives according to natural rather than spiritual things. It is worth taking a moment here to look at what wars with our spirit and keeps us from living every day in the ways of God. What is "self"? What is our "flesh"?

The Bible tells us that people have three parts: spirit, soul, and body. I believe that in the soul rests the seat of the mind, will, and emotions. In this sense, to state it simply, our spirit is the part of ourselves that connects to God and is the "branch" through which spiritual fruit grows in our lives. If this branch is grafted into Jesus, we are very fruitful; if not, our fruit is worthless and should be cut away.[7] The flesh, then, is our body that touches the natural/physical world. It is the seat of our hormones, if you will, that makes us lust after other things; the part of us that touches and appreciates material wealth; the part of us that interacts with the world around us. In this sense it is where our sin nature is, because it defines itself only by the created and not the Creator— it is the part of us that would like to believe that the physical world is all there is, so why not enjoy everything it has to offer without restraint! Why not be given over to the lusts of our eyes? Why not fight for our own rights and give in to our jealousies?

> If ye have bitter envying and strife in your hearts, glory not, and lie not against the truth. This wisdom descendeth not from above, but is *earthly, sensual* [or *natural*], devilish. For where envying and strife is, there is confusion and every evil work. (James 3:14–16)

This is what our sin nature (or flesh) encourages us to do: to envy, to strive with others, to be wrathful, and to walk in the other "works of the flesh."[8]

Then, as many see it, there is the soul, caught in the middle between the flesh and the spirit, struggling to choose what is right. This is the "I" Paul speaks of in Romans 7, the self: the mind, will, and emotions of a person that struggles between the flesh and the spirit.

> I don't understand myself at all, for I really want to do what is right, but I don't do it. Instead, I do the very thing I hate. I know perfectly well that what I am doing is wrong, and my bad conscience shows that I agree that the law is good. But I can't help myself, because it is *sin inside me* [my *flesh*] that makes me do these evil things.
>
> I know I am rotten through and through so far as *my old sinful nature* [my *flesh*] is concerned. No matter which way I turn, I can't make myself do right. I [my soul] want to, but I can't. When I want to do good, I don't. And when I try not to do wrong, I do it anyway. But if I am doing what I don't want to do, I am not really the one doing it; the *sin within me* [my *flesh*] is doing it.
>
> It seems to be a fact of life that when I want to do what

is right, I inevitably do what is wrong. I love God's law with all *my heart* [my *spirit*]. But there is *another law* [my *sin nature within my flesh*] at work within *me* that is at war *with my mind* [my *self*]. This law wins the fight and makes me a slave to the sin that is still within me. Oh, what a miserable person I am! Who will free me from this life that is dominated by sin? (Romans 7:15–25 NLT)

It is like the age-old parable we see in so many stories: On one shoulder sits a little devil and on the other sits a little angel; in the middle is our head—trying to decide and reason out what we should do. The self is trying to do what is right but is so strongly attracted to do what is wrong. Do we put Jesus on the throne, or sin? The choice to do what is godly seems so obvious, but the attraction to do what is wrong feels so right! It is as if there is a continuum through the self from the spiritual to the natural—a supernatural tug-of-war with self as the rope in the middle, and God on one end and Satan on the other, pulling in opposite directions. There we are, tugged back and forth, to the point we feel we may tear in half! What hope have we? What can we possibly do?

As usual, what we need to do is see this struggle the way God does, not the way humankind has pictured it all these years. Paul did not end this discussion with "Oh, what a miserable person I am!" (see next page).

"Self" must be redefined. If "self" is our "I"—that core within us that makes our decisions and defines who we are, what we think, and how we act—then self is not so much evil as it is confused. If it were simple, it would just be a matter of saying that the "self" that chooses evil is evil and the "self" that chooses good is good—we either obey the little devil or the little angel. But the problem is that self is clouded in self-doubt, self-esteem, self-criticism, self-deception, self-this, self-that, and self-the-other! Self is truly so wrapped up in itself that it tends to pay little attention to good or evil and simply acts to preserve its own self-definition. Forget trying to listen to the advice of the little devil or the little angel—"self" is just trying to survive! (As if we actually had the time to sit down and make every decision consciously.) Most of the time we just act according to preconditioned thinking and patterns we have been forming from the day we were born.

Most of us have little joy in our lives because joy has very little to do with our self-concept. "Self" has been defined by culture, background, and our environment—wild vines we have grafted ourselves into regardless of the fruit they bear—and self-preservation is the rule of the day. Satan doesn't have to influence us to do evil or keep us from God—he just has to keep us so busy that we continue to act out of habit rather than cutting off the bad and grafting ourselves into Jesus!

The devil is not the problem. The problem is that our selves cannot draw vitality from anything except Jesus! Without this vitality, how can we ever hope to resist the ever-so-attractive desires of our flesh?

Look at what Paul went on to say immediately after the hopeless passage we just discussed in Romans 7:

> Thank God! *The answer is in Jesus Christ our Lord. . . . There is no condemnation for those who belong to Christ Jesus.* For the power of the life-giving Spirit has freed you through Christ Jesus from the power of sin that leads to death. . . . He sent his own Son in a human body like ours, except that ours are sinful. God destroyed sin's control over us by giving his Son as a sacrifice for our sins. He did this so that the requirement of the law would be fully accomplished for us *who no longer follow our sinful nature but instead follow the Spirit.* (Romans 7:25–8:4 NLT)

We need to change our self-concept from sin-consciousness to Christ-consciousness! We need to stop defining self from our pasts, our cultures, and our natural worlds—measuring ourselves by ourselves and defining *good* by looking at those around us and saying, "Well, at least I am not like that person!"[9]—and start defining ourselves by the standard of Jesus. That, of course, will take some self-awareness—self-awareness that will only come from remaining close to Jesus, open and vulnerable in His light until we are changed into His likeness. We must know Him, be one with Him, and then we can enter into His joy.

But here is the clincher: God sees it differently. His idea is not that spirit, soul, and body are a continuum (soul or self caught in the middle and being pulled in two directions at once between the spiritual and the natural) but rather a conduit—taking power, strength, and life from the spirit and passing it through the soul into the physical realm. We should be pipelines through which the Holy Spirit can manifest the kingdom of God, allowing His will to be done on earth as it is in heaven, not indecisive, confused egos caught in a tug-of-war between the natural and the supernatural.

Joy Does Not Depend on Circumstances

Some years ago I was honored to share a meal with Richard Wurmbrand, a former prisoner of the communists, who endured severe torture for his faith. I asked if he ever felt like he was losing his mind. He said he did but that he gave it to Christ so he didn't have to worry anymore. When he suffered heartache for his family, he gave his emotions to Christ as well, and he was free. Then he gave his body to Christ and no longer needed to worry about his health. Armed with complete death to his flesh, the communists could no longer hurt him.

"The guard came for me one day and said, 'You must realize that I can break your arms, your legs, anything I want?' " Richard told me. "And I answered him, 'If you break my arm, I will say, *God loves you,* and if you break my leg, I will say, *I love you, too.*' With that, the guard began to cry, and I was able to lead him to Christ that day."

When we're grafted into Jesus, what shall we fear?

Perhaps this is why Jesus often encouraged:

Blessed [happy] are ye, when men shall hate you, and when they shall separate you from their company, and shall reproach you, and cast out your name as evil, for the Son of man's sake. Rejoice ye in that day, and *leap for joy*: for, behold, your reward is great in heaven: for in the like manner did their fathers unto the prophets. (Luke 6:22–23)

This was the joy Paul and Silas had while in prison in Philippi. They rejoiced in the Lord with stripes on their backs and stocks on their feet in the pit of an ancient Roman jail.[10] How many of us can say our situations have ever been lower than that? Then what room do we have to be so glum? . . . *unless we simply are* not *walking out the plan of God in our lives!*

Peter talked of the joy set before us, even in the face of persecution or whatever circumstances might bring, in this way:

> So be truly glad! *There is wonderful joy ahead,* even though it is necessary for you to endure many trials for a while.
>
> These trials are only to test your faith, to show that it is strong and pure. It is being tested as fire tests and purifies gold—and your faith is far more precious to God than mere gold. So if your faith remains strong after being tried by fiery trials, it will bring you much praise and glory and honor on the day when Jesus Christ is revealed to the whole world.
>
> You love him even though you have never seen him. Though you do not see him, you trust him; and *even now you are happy with a glorious, inexpressible joy.* Your reward for trusting him will be the salvation of your souls. (1 Peter 1:6–9 NLT)

Persecutions will come in the world in one way or another— we know this, because even those of us not out actively telling others about Jesus experience hardships and trials. Why not instead take such things head on and have Jesus' joy through them? Accept God's Word, walk in it, and obey His voice—He will never leave us or forsake us![11] After all, what can separate us from His love?[12] We Christians have no reason to be despondent and full of worry, *for the joy of our Lord Jesus is our strength!*

Always be full of joy in the Lord. I say it again—rejoice! Let everyone see that you are considerate in all you do. Remember, the Lord is coming soon. Don't worry about anything; instead, pray about everything. Tell God what you need, and thank him for all he has done. If you do this, you will experience God's peace, which is far more wonderful than the human mind can understand. His peace will guard your hearts and minds as you live in Christ Jesus. (Philippians 4:4–7 NLT)

CHAPTER FIVE

Free From Evil

Thou shouldest keep them from evil.

JOHN 17:15

The world seems more full of evil today than ever before. At the turn of the twenty-first century we are not marked by the futuristic utopia we had envisioned for this era. I began my ministry in the early '70s, just a few years after we had first landed on the moon. At that time we looked ahead to the new millennium with starry-eyed wonder at what technology and the sciences would accomplish. Yet now we live in a time dominated by more fear, stress, and anxiety than we did during the protests just before the end of the Vietnam War. We seem to be bearing the fruit of a society that planted self-sufficiency and pride deeply in our hearts as we bought the biggest lie the devil has ever told: that we can go it alone without God.

If we think that humanity has truly progressed throughout our history, we need to take a careful look at the fruit of the last century. In a time when we thought the world was growing more open-minded and accepting of other beliefs and cultures, we saw more Christians killed for their faith than in the previous 1,900 years combined. In fact, nearly 65 percent of all the martyrs that have died since Jesus were murdered in the last one hundred years.[1]

In the wake of this "age of understanding," the twenty-first century began with fear that the very technology we had put our hope in would backfire on us—remember the Y2K scare? Then the terrorist attacks of September 11, 2001, exposed our vulnerability to those with hatred in their hearts. And as if this were not enough, our economy and stock market are still reeling from people who lied to us again and again about the value of their companies to push up the prices of their stocks—and personal portfolios—while their actions drove those same companies to bankruptcy. Twenty-four-hour news channels fill us in on every detail of such crises while also circulating the news of wars and rumors of war that Jesus prophesied would come. Cinema and television are no longer satisfied with "good guys always win" stories—now the heroes of some of the most popular series and films are mobsters, homosexuals, witches and warlocks, thieves, and serial killers. Even the "good guys" have serious character flaws and dark sides. Moral and ethical issues are clouded by in-depth news reports and talk shows. "What is right?" is a question with more differing opinions than ever before. There have also been more cults and new religions birthed in the last century than in all the rest of history combined.

How are we who are devoted to Jesus supposed to live and raise our children in a world that seems so headed for hell?

"Lord, Keep Us From Evil"

In John 17:15, Jesus prayed that we should be kept from evil, but with evil seemingly so solidly entrenched around us, what are we to do? Do we just shut ourselves off from the world, turn off the TV and radio, and live like we are in a monastery? While this may seem the only way, the truth is, that would not even help us. If we are going to separate ourselves from evil, we must dig it up at its roots and cast it out of our lives.

The problem is that the real root of evil is not from outside of us but from within. *Before we can deal with society's evils, we must deal with our own.*

Evil doesn't begin with adultery, murder, bank robbery, fraud, or genocide. Evil starts with lives that are empty of God. It starts with boredom. It starts with thinking that we deserve more out of life, and no one is going to help us get it besides ourselves. It breeds where people are determined that they want a certain thing and the only way they are going to get it is by following their own desires. They don't know God. They think God is not really interested in them anyway, so why should they bother to know Him? They think they are better off without God's guidance or help. Then evil builds as they give in more and more to their selfish, fleshly desires and redefine "good" to fit their own self-concepts.

Jesus described how evil can come into our lives and grow to take over, blinding us to the truth:

> Your eye is a lamp for your body. A pure eye lets sunshine into your soul. But an evil eye shuts out the light and plunges you into darkness. If the light you think you have is really darkness, how deep that darkness will be! (Matthew 6:22–23 NLT)

What we set our eyes upon determines our focus in life. If we have a pure focus (the King James Version says "single" here, perhaps contrasting with the "double mindedness" expressed in James 1:6–8) on the truth, then we will have the light of God in our lives. Rejection of God's truth is fertile soil for evil.

If we are focused on half-truths and accept them as whole truths, how great is the darkness that grows within our hearts! Why would we accept half-truths? *Because they justify our self-concepts more than the Word of God does.* They let us live as we want to, justifying our lifestyles and our lack of intimacy with God. By accepting these half-truths as full truths, we don't have to change, and we continue with a "good" that is defined by the self on the throne of our lives, refusing to measure ourselves against the example of Jesus and allowing Him to order our steps.

If we examine what Jesus is talking about in this passage, we can recognize even more clearly the source of evil:

Don't store up treasures here on earth, where they can be eaten by moths and get rusty, and where thieves break in and steal. Store your treasures in heaven, where they will never become moth-eaten or rusty and where they will be safe from thieves. Wherever your treasure is, there your heart and thoughts will also be. . . . No one can serve two masters. For you will hate one and love the other, or be devoted to one and despise the other. You cannot serve both God and money. . . . He will give you all you need from day to day if you live for him and make the Kingdom of God your primary concern. (Matthew 6:19–21, 24, 33 NLT)

Taken at a glance, you might think that while Jesus was giving a discourse on God's provision and how we should not love money, He inserts this little rabbit trail about evil and then returns to His discourse on finances. But I don't think Jesus was changing the subject here at all. Throughout the entire passage He is talking about how God provides for His children.

Remember how we said that evil comes from wanting something that you feel life is cheating you out of and deciding that the only way you can get it is to look out for your own interests? Well, that is what Jesus is talking about here. When you want something, how do you plan on getting it? Are you going to turn to the world's system of accumulating wealth, popularity, job security, material goods, or whatever it is you are after? You think if you have those things you will be happy—or have joy—and so you focus on acquiring those things you have set your heart on. Within that focus, you will eventually be willing to cut some corners to get your desire.

For those who don't call themselves Christians, this may seem obvious, but I am not talking about those outside of the church. I am talking to those that do call Jesus "Lord." We attend church regularly, we call ourselves Christians, and we think we belong to Christ, but our "eye" (focus) is double. With our mouths we give allegiance to God, while in our hearts we are not after God and His kingdom but worldly wealth. We really don't believe that following God will get us everything that will make us happy, so we fellowship with other "believers" who feel the same way. We compare ourselves to others, vainly thinking that we are at least better or smarter than most of the people who sit next to us in the pews because we have memorized more Scripture, pray more, lead a Bible study, or some other such religious work. We may even pray in tongues, cast out demons, or lead others to the Lord on a regular basis, but if we treasure the things of this world more than the things of the kingdom of God and then create doctrines to justify those desires in our own mind, we leave an unsanctified self on the throne of our lives—and how great is the darkness in our souls! We call Jesus "Lord, Lord," but when God impresses on us to do something to help manifest His kingdom on the earth, we don't even hear it because we are so wrapped up in our own *selves*!

> Not all people who sound religious are really godly. They may refer to me as "Lord," but they still won't enter the Kingdom of Heaven. *The decisive issue is whether they obey my Father in heaven.* On judgment day many will tell me, "Lord, Lord, we prophesied in your name and cast out demons in your name and performed many miracles in your name." But I will reply, "I never knew you. Go away; the things you did were unauthorized" (Matthew 7:21–23 NLT).

Look at *Harper's Bible Dictionary*'s definition of "evil":

> All forms of evil are regarded as ultimately occasioned by *the disobedience and rebellion of the human race with regard to God and God's will.* Evil occurs where and when God's will is hindered by human sin.[2]

We may be building churches and ministries and kingdoms in His name, but do these things come out of time spent getting to know Jesus, receiving His plans, and walking in them? Or have we set our eyes on the good things that can go along with such organizations—the wealth, the reputation, the respect—and in truth gone about using God's name to build these kingdoms for ourselves? Are we truly acting in obedience to the Jesus we know through prayer and His Word, or are we simply trying to justify our *selves* by walking religiously before other people? Are we defining our self-worth by the standards of His Word or by the accepted practices of our cultures and local churches? Is our Christianity based on Jesus or on a conservative American-Christian culture that makes us think we know better than everyone else? How do I know people like this exist in the body of Christ? Because I have been there!

> *Are we defining our self-worth by the standards of His Word or by the accepted practices of our cultures and local churches?*

On one visit to the White House in the '80s, President Reagan invited me to step into the Oval Office. There he showed me the Bible used for the swearing-in ceremony at his inauguration. It was opened to 2 Chronicles 7:14. There was a note in the margin that read, "Son, this scripture is for the healing of the nations." A plaque on his desk read, "A man can become too great in his own eyes to be used by God." Boy, did I feel important!

But the president didn't stop there. He allowed me to walk with him as he went into the Rose Garden. A crowd of reporters waiting behind a roped-off area began to shout at him and to take photos. I felt drunk on my own importance. I had been invited many times to the White House and realized I was one of about one hundred ministers in the nation to have had this privilege.

The president was asking me questions. I was advising him. I thought, "It is so great to have the president of the United States as a friend." With that thought, he turned to me, shook my hand, and said, "Good to see you again, Bob."

What a blow! What was I doing there? At the time it mattered more to me that the president knew my name than that Jesus did. Boy, did I have my wires crossed! My own selfish desires to be famous were sliding me into the evil of hypocrisy.

The Root of *All* Evil

Paul warned Timothy about the source of all evil: "*The love of money is the root of all evil*: which while some coveted after, they have erred from the faith, and pierced themselves through with many sorrows" (1 Timothy 6:10).

Vine's tells us that the Greek for "love of money" is *philarguria* (literally "the love of silver"), which means "covetous, avaricious."[3] If I may be so bold, it means simply "selfishness"—*selfishness* (self-on-the-throne-ish-ness) is the root of *all evil*. The *New Bible Dictionary* has a similar definition for "evil":

> The Hebrew word comes from a root meaning "to spoil," "to break in pieces": being broken and so made worthless. It is essentially what is unpleasant, disagreeable, offensive. The word binds together the evil deed and its consequences. In the New Testament, *kakos* and *ponçros* mean respectively the quality of evil in its essential character, and its hurtful effects or influence. It is used in both physical and moral senses. While these aspects are different, there is frequently a close relationship between them. Much physical evil is due to moral evil: suffering and sin are not necessarily connected in individual cases, but *human selfishness and sin explain much of the world's ills.*[4]

First Timothy 6:10 tells us that those who fall into this trap "erred" in their faith. The footnote in my Bible tells me that "erred" also means "been deceived." *Those who walk in selfishness deceive themselves into believing that their ways are right.* Their eyes are darkened, and they see everything through a lying filter of self-justification.

"There is a way which seemeth right unto a man, but the end thereof are the ways of death" (Proverbs 14:12).

Look at how *The Message* paraphrases what Paul is talking about only a few verses earlier:

> If you have leaders . . . who refuse the solid words of our Master Jesus and this godly instruction, tag them for

what they are: ignorant windbags who infect the air with germs of envy, controversy, bad-mouthing, suspicious rumors. Eventually there's an epidemic of backstabbing, and *truth is but a distant memory*. They think religion is a way to make a fast buck. A devout life does bring wealth, but it's *the rich simplicity of being yourself before God*. (1 Timothy 6:3–6)

The only solution is to go to Jesus and let Him heal our blindness!

Search me, O God, and know my heart: try me, and know my thoughts: And see if there be any wicked way in me, and lead me in the way everlasting. (Psalm 139:23–24)

Are We Living Under Deception?

Most of us will never commit a felony—and in this we think we are all right! Instead we sink down into a soothing lukewarmness that is neither a force for heaven nor a threat to hell. We grow more and more tolerant and complacent, satisfied to live "entertained" rather than fulfilled. We watch evil flourish on the news, thinking unconsciously, *Well, at least I'm not that bad*—then turn the channel to a sports event or a sitcom to numb the Spirit within us that urges us to pray and get God's plan for our world. The Bible calls it "searing our consciences":

But the Spirit explicitly says that in later times some will fall away from the faith, paying attention to deceitful spirits and doctrines of demons, by means of the hypocrisy of liars *seared in their own conscience* as with a branding iron. (1 Timothy 4:1–2 NASB)

We become content to live in our religiosity, content to know all our church's catch phrases and "correct answers," which we can rattle off at the drop of a hat. But we don't really know God or His purpose for our lives. We are in reality building our own kingdoms rather than manifesting His. Just like the religious leaders of Jesus' time on earth, we are so content to live in a reality void of God's grace and miracle-working, life-changing power that if anyone comes across our path preaching the true gospel, we would rather call him a heretic or false prophet than change ourselves to align with the truth.

It might seem logical to interpret the line in the Lord's Prayer "Deliver us from evil" as a request that nothing bad would happen to us, but we forget that it is preceded by "Lead us not into temptation."[5] Evil is not on the earth so much to hurt others (which is the world's perspective of evil): "Hey, if I am not hurting anyone else, what's the problem?" Its real purpose is to separate us from God. Evil's true

> *We have lost our confidence to stand up for Jesus because what is in the world around us seems more real to us than Jesus does.*

intent is to keep us from knowing God, being one with Jesus, and living a life of His present-day ministry through the power of the Holy Spirit. Satan would just as soon have an ineffective, hypocritical Christian walking the earth as he would have a serial killer plaguing a community, because *the hypocritical Christian is actually more efficient in driving people away from God and toward hell.*

It Is Our Lukewarmness That Has Changed Our Nation

We have lost our confidence to stand up for Jesus because what is in the world around us seems more real to us than Jesus does. We don't *know* Him anymore! We are numb to the reality of God because we spend much if not all of our time focused on things of the world. What the "experts" say seems more real and relevant than what the Bible says. It is time to renew our minds to what the Bible says and let God show us its relevance!

The dictionary definition for *hypocrisy* is "a feigning to be what one is not or to believe what one does not."[6] But I also like to look at it this way, breaking it down into its parts: *hypo* means "under" (as *hypodermic* needle means a needle that goes "under the skin"), and -*crisy* comes from the same word as "critic," meaning that we are "judging" or "evaluating." In the same way that "under construction" means something that is not finished but is still being built, to me, *hypocrisy* means that our beliefs are still "under evaluation"—we are still thinking about it and have not yet truly decided what we really believe.

It is time to get off the fence and decide! If the world system is truth, then follow it, but if God is truth, then follow Him!

If we don't have the time to get alone with Jesus and let Him develop within us the conviction of His truth and His kingdom, we have no right to call Him "Lord" and think we have any claim to His salvation!

> *It is our complacency and lack of biblical conviction for truth that is letting our world go to hell.*

It is our complacency and lack of biblical conviction for truth that is letting our world go to hell. America has moved from the fifth- to the third-largest mission field in the world. We have the resources, but we're losing ground. Literally 90 percent of all offerings are spent here, and we have fifty-seven million confessing Christians who could easily evangelize the entire country. Yet we're rising steadily on the list of the most unchurched, unevangelized people on earth.

Today when we see churches hold "revivals," we mistakenly think we're seeing America revived. However, we have to acknowledge that many of us are busy managing our programs and projects, looking back wistfully at what God did, content to glory over how Christ's power was manifest in a bygone era instead of permitting Christ to accomplish His work in our time.

The world has, in many ways, taken over the church. Until "self" is dethroned and Christ is enthroned in our hearts, the church—made up of God's people—will continue taking two steps backward for every one step forward. We watch the same entertainment, wear the same clothes, laugh at many of the same jokes, and share the same appetites for fashion, food, and fun as the world does. The world has infected, seduced, polluted, and brainwashed us with its entertainment, styles, and lusts. Christian children often dress like gang members and foul-mouthed singers. Christian women sometimes wear styles inspired by the homosexual fashion world. We never even ask what motivates our trends in clothing or entertainment.

How can a Christian teach Sunday school in the morning and then go to an afternoon movie with graphic violence, nudity, the name of Christ profaned, and filthy language and sit there placidly eating popcorn with his wife and children? How can we sing in the choir, greet the visitors, and then go home that night to channel surf, watch the most despicable perversions, then click off the TV, read our Bible for ten minutes, say a prayer, and never feel any conviction for our behavior? We wonder why we're having problems in our lives, in our homes, and with our children. It is because our *flesh is on the throne*. When we surrender to the flesh, we live in a state of neutrality and appeasement instead of righteousness and holiness.

We may boast that God is moving in our churches. He's moving all right—moving right out the door!

William J. Bennett, in *The Death of Outrage,* scolds Americans for allowing their president at the time, William Clinton, to "defile" the office of the presidency by using it as a gimmick to get girls. Instead of rising in outrage against the blatant immorality of social and political leaders, some Christians defend the guilty, while most are silent. The Senate didn't have the conviction to remove Clinton from office because many of them were absorbed in the same sin. Some wondered, "What's the big deal?" Others were apathetic, because it didn't seem to affect them personally. We don't usually fight until something infringes on our own individual rights or those of a loved one. Thus, for us, morality isn't the issue. Personal comfort is. Why get worked up about something if it doesn't directly touch us in some way?

But we cannot expect the nation to be more moral than we are. I am here to tell you, *as goes the church, so goes the nation.* There's been little outrage over tens of millions of abortions, over the profusion of Internet pornography, or over a divorce rate that affects more than half the population. There is as little outrage over the massive number of teenage pregnancies and suicides in the church as there is outside of it. We've grown accustomed to alcohol and drug abuse in our midst—or else we are simply turning a blind eye to it, hoping it will go away because we are too busy being entertained to get involved.

We have no conviction to do right and stand up for God's kingdom because we haven't been with Jesus!

Where's the outrage at more Christians being persecuted worldwide today than at any other time in history?

Where's the outrage at more Christians being persecuted worldwide today than at any other time in history? Where's the outrage over thirty-four million people dying of AIDS? Where is a Christian's outrage about fatherlessness?

Over twenty-seven million American children will go to sleep tonight without a father in their home. Ninety-two percent of the young people in the city of New York have never even darkened the door of a church. A quarter million high-school girls get pregnant every year. One in eight babies are born outside of wedlock. America leads the world per capita in sexually active teenagers and in abortions.

We show little outrage as states and denominations fight to approve homosexual marriages and lobby to lower the age of sexual consent—in essence legalizing child molestation. Little outrage is heard over hardcore pornography, which represents a larger consumer market than Hollywood moviemaking. There is little outrage over crime, even though every twenty-two seconds in the U.S. a major crime occurs, and every thirty-four minutes that crime is a murder. One hundred thousand students carry guns into classrooms on any given day, and one in five American children will end up in jail. One million teenagers in America are alcoholics. America leads the industrial world in murder, rape, abortion, and incarceration. Where is our outrage?

Television shows such as *Joe Millionaire* became top-ranked in America because instant gratification appeals to our greed. Reality shows receive high ratings because they can get women into skimpy clothing and compromising situations or put people in dangerous, disgusting, or vulgar settings for our "entertainment." TV has learned to appeal to the lusts of our flesh to get a bigger audience—and people are flocking to it! Satan is taking over our airwaves with little more than a peep from the church. Why? Because as many of us rush home to watch these shows as people in the world do.

This is the spiritual poverty that Mother Teresa spoke to me about so many years ago. As the most powerful nation on earth we have used our position to become comfortable at the expense of a lost and dying world. The church was to be the light of the world, yet it is obvious our Christian "light" no longer dispels the darkness. If this is true, once again, how great is our own darkness! No wonder 80 percent of our young people leave the church when they leave home. They saw that it didn't work for their parents, so why would it work for them?

It Is Time to Be Jesus-Justified Instead of Self-Justified

It is very difficult to fault the media for providing us with the form of entertainment that *we want,* nor can we reasonably fault immoral politicians that *we elect*! Though many may not agree with this, you cannot completely legislate morality. More legislation leads to more work for our police forces and legal system. All we can expect is more of the same in this world until who we are in Jesus so affects those around us that they turn off the filth and demand more of God for themselves!

And the only way that will ever come to pass is if we put God's ways and God's Word above our own.

If evil comes from selfishness, then it is time to replace that selfishness with Christlikeness. Are we willing to love others with the love of Jesus? Are we willing to look to God as our Source for all we need and want, or will we stick to the world's ways to find satisfaction? Are we willing to bless those who curse us, placing the demand on God to justify us rather than trying to justify ourselves, or will we file suit? The only way God can ever "keep us from evil" is if we walk closely to Him in every area of our lives.

Richard Wurmbrand once said, "As the Communist atheists [my persecutors] allowed no place for Jesus in their hearts, I decided I would leave not the smallest place for Satan in mine." If we are ever to be a threat to evil, we must have the same conviction!

CHAPTER SIX

The Truth Shall Set You Free

Sanctify them through thy truth: thy word is truth.

JOHN 17:17

The young prostitute—caught in the very act, they had said—must have looked very bewildered into Jesus' eyes that day as He told her simply, "Neither do I condemn you. Go and sin no more."[1]

I always imagined that she stood there for a moment, still shuddering, holding her torn dress to cover herself, unsure of what to do. She probably looked questioningly at Jesus for a moment, then stole a glance at her former accusers, none of whom remained, though just moments before they had been ready to play judge, jury, and executioner over her. She might have stolen away as quickly as possible, delivered from a torturous death by a man brave enough to confront others with the truth of their own sins. I imagine that these men began to turn their attention

> *She might have stolen away as quickly as possible, delivered from a torturous death by a man brave enough to confront others with the truth of their own sins.*

again toward Jesus, ready to redirect their original murderous intent.

Yet despite their obvious attitude of menace, Jesus wasn't through revealing to them that the darkness in their own hearts was far blacker than that of the worst prostitute's. Soon He said,

> "I am the world's Light. No one who follows me stumbles around in the darkness. I provide plenty of light to live in."

The Pharisees objected, "All we have is your word on this. We need more than this to go on."

Jesus replied, "You're right that you only have my word. But you can depend on it being true. I know where I've come from and where I go next. You don't know where I'm from or where I'm headed. *You decide according to what you can see and touch. I don't make judgments like that. But even if I did, my judgment would be true because I wouldn't make it out of the narrowness of my experience but in the largeness of the One who sent me, the Father.* That fulfills the conditions set down in God's Law: that you can count on the testimony of two witnesses. And that is what you have: You have my word and you have the word of the Father who sent me."

They said, "Where is this so-called Father of yours?"

Jesus said, "You're looking right at me and you don't see me. How do you expect to see the Father? *If you knew me, you would at the same time know the Father. . . .*

"You're tied down to the mundane; I'm in touch with what is beyond your horizons. You live in terms of what you see and touch. I'm living on other terms. I told you that you were missing God in all this. You're at a dead end. If you won't believe I am who I say I am, you're at the dead end of sins. *You're missing God in your lives. . . .*

"When you raise up the Son of Man, then you will know who I am—that *I'm not making this up, but speaking only what the Father taught me.* The One who sent me stays with me. He doesn't abandon me. He sees how much joy I take in pleasing him."

When he put it in these terms, many people decided to believe.

Then Jesus turned to the Jews who had claimed to believe in him. *"If you stick with this, living out what I tell you, you are my disciples for sure. Then you will experience for yourselves the truth, and the truth will free you"* (John 8:12–19, 23–24, 28–32 THE MESSAGE).

Unable to reach beyond their selves, many never received this truth that Jesus was so freely offering. They remained trapped in their traditions and customs. What Jesus was teaching was outside the field of answers they had memorized eagerly at Pharisee school, thinking that always having the "correct" answer was their ticket to salvation. In fact, they were more bewildered than ever, not because Jesus gave different answers, but because He was asking different questions.

Jesus was coming to them with something new, though it was buried in every chapter of the holy writings of their covenant: *It is not so much what you do as it is Who you know and obey.* They wanted to justify themselves by their opinions and actions, keeping the outward commandments to be seen by others but

> *They didn't want to know God but to control, dictate, and be worshiped of men themselves.*

ignoring the inward heart issues of truly following God. They were ready to judge and condemn others for falling short of their standard so that all would see their uncompromising dedication to their principles, yet when the very God whom they said they obeyed walked right into their midst, their self-justifications blinded them: They didn't even recognize Him. They didn't want to know God but to control, dictate, and be worshiped of men themselves. Entrapped by sin, they claimed to be free, but here was Jesus before them, presenting the truth with such clarity and sincerity that it became a stumbling block—a crushing stone—upon which they would either build their salvation or beneath which they would be smashed in their own self-righteousness.

Meeting the Truth in person left them no other options.[2]

Are we in our churches today more like those who accepted Jesus' light and saw what was truly in their heart or more like the Pharisees who clung to their own traditions, opinions, and other half-truths rather than having to change their self-righteous self-concepts? Are we just as wrapped up in our own beliefs, cultures, and desires as they were? Do we justify ourselves by learning all the "correct" responses while missing the real Answer? Are we satisfied with looking good to others while Jesus stands nearby, grieving at our ignorance of Him?

> *Do we justify ourselves by learning all the "correct" responses while missing the real Answer?*

It is time we got to really know the Truth and let that Truth set us free from our selves.

The Truth Will Set *You* Free

Jesus' fifth unanswered prayer was "That they also might be sanctified through the truth."[3] The "sanctification" Jesus speaks of here is the process of being "set apart for God . . . to make a person or thing the opposite of *koinos,* 'common.' "[4] According to Peter, we are called to be a "peculiar [special or uncommon] people, that ye should shew forth the praises of him who hath called you out of darkness into his marvellous light."[5] Jesus called us the salt of the earth, the light of the world, and a city set on a hill that cannot be hidden.[6] Christians should be obvious to others because we speak and act differently. We carry God's light with us. When we enter a room there should be a different atmosphere because we bring the Holy Spirit with us.

A few years ago another evangelical leader and I were invited to meet with the president of the United States. We flew together to Washington and stayed at the Hilton Hotel. As my colleague stepped through the doorway, a precious woman who was vacuuming the lobby looked at him and instantly started weeping. She fell to her knees, with probably no less than twenty people looking at her, raised her hands, and cried, "God, forgive me, I'm a fornicator."

God's presence changes things, so if He is truly in us, then His life-changing power should shine through us! Yet often we are indistinguishable from the rest of the people in the world. Some might call themselves "undercover Christians," but the truth is, we're not undercover, we're under-changed!

Nothing can blind us to this more than ego, self-deception, or dead religion. Sometimes those who seem to be "doing the most for God" are also the most blinded. In the past three decades, scandals have rocked the church on an international scale with every vice from greed to adultery to child molestation. Then, as if this were not enough, on the other side have been those of us who stand in judgment over these people, erring on the side of stiff religiosity and driving even more away from God because of our unforgiveness and self-righteous demeanor. Believe me, I know what I am talking about here—I have experienced this fleshly pride firsthand.

During the scandal surrounding the demise of the PTL television network in the mid-1980s, news programs such as *Crossfire, Nightline,* and others invited me to debate. Charles Gibson on *Good Morning, America* continued one such show through two extra segments because we were having such a good "discussion." I thought I was doing a service to the body of Christ, but instead I was engaging in what evangelist Doug Stringer calls the "Spiritual Immune-Deficiency Disease"—*cells eating other cells within the body.*

I've wasted a lot of energy over the years seeking the approval of others, becoming intoxicated by someone else's power, working as an unofficial arbitrator in big-name church cases, and engaging in media fistfights all over the nation. I thought I had arrived and was finally really

> *I've wasted a lot of energy over the years seeking the approval of others.*

doing something to help Jesus. But Jesus doesn't need such help—He needs my humble obedience. I wasn't carrying out His ministry on the earth—I was exalting my flesh-blinded self! I was seeking validation and justification for my flesh; I was allowing flesh to fight other flesh—and all under a Christian banner!

> *Like those drunk with wine, those of us drunk with flesh are unreasonable and bleary-eyed.*

Like those drunk with wine, those of us drunk with flesh are unreasonable and bleary-eyed. We do not see things clearly or truthfully but rather as we want to see them, through the haziness of self-centeredness. We can go on like this our whole lives unless we are "arrested" for a DUI: Deceived Under the Influence of our flesh. We as Christians have a choice at that point: We can either get real with God and let Him sober us up, or we can choose to cling to the deception that has so entranced us. If we cling to such deception, we become poster children for the devil—Christians trying to live out Christianity by the power of the flesh rather than the power of the Spirit.

As I was initially pulling together my thoughts for this book, I met a businessman who people said was the godliest man in town. He was small and wiry, in his mid-forties, with slightly graying temples. He wore a tailored suit that matched his refined manners. We had a long drive together through traffic from one part of the city to another, so I spent the time telling him and three other ministers in the van about some of the things I wanted to discuss in this book.

I noticed in a few minutes that the businessman had become completely silent, his face slowly turning ashen. Finally he exploded, "God help me! I'm all messed up!" He motioned, with tears streaming down his face, for the driver to pull off the freeway.

"That's me!" he cried as he paced beside the van. "That's me. I can't live the Christian life. I've tried to do everything right, but I can't."

This was a Holy Spirit arrest! Through the power of the Holy Spirit present with us in that car, he came to a point of clearly seeing the truth. Cut to the heart, he accepted it, confessed his sin, and chose to walk more closely with Jesus than ever before. The truth can have that kind of effect on people—suddenly seeing the truth clearly set him free of his own hypocrisy!

Are We Blinded to the Truth?

When Pilate tried Jesus, they had the following conversation:

Pilate . . . said to Him, "So You are a king?" Jesus answered, "You say correctly that I am a king. For this I have been born, and for this I have come into the world, to bear witness to the truth. Everyone who is of the truth hears My voice." Pilate said to Him, "What is truth?" (John 18:37–38 NASB).

With Truth himself standing before him and reaching out to him, Pilate asked the question that has spawned all human philosophy, theology, and, unfortunately, religion.[7] In the very face of Truth, Pilate rejected Truth, desiring rather to hang on to his own opinions and "political correctness" rather than risk embracing the Truth and thus offending either the Roman pagans or the Jewish priests. He was too absorbed in protecting his own self-interests and position—too trapped by His own self-concept—to accept the Truth that would set Him free. Thus, the imprisoned and enslaved always condemn the free, because the truth they offer is more than the self-absorbed and self-deceived are able to bear.

The imprisoned and enslaved always condemn the free, because the truth they offer is more than the self-absorbed and self-deceived are able to bear.

Jesus experienced this with the Jewish leaders as well as with

Pilate, just as those who have struggled for a real relationship with God have always experienced it from the religious leaders of their day, which is one of the reasons the body of Christ is so divided today. We have forgotten to be hungry for truth and have grown satisfied with repeating our self-made doctrines rather than bowing our knees in unity and seeking God for the whole truth. It is time that we become so hungry for the truth that we will let nothing else satisfy us or get in the way of manifesting His truth on earth.

But perhaps we are stuck with Pilate in this, for we need to answer the same question he asked—what is truth?—and be very clear about the answer. It is easy in the highest sense to say that the best definition of truth is that Jesus is Truth personified.[8] Only by truly knowing Him can we know the truth. The truths of the entire universe are tied up in knowing Jesus, for through Him all things are revealed as they actually are: "I am the light of the world: he that followeth me shall not walk in darkness, but shall have the light of life" (John 8:12).

The nature of light is that in it we see every nuance and detail of things clearly. Jewelers use a magnifying glass and a bright light to examine diamonds for even the tiniest flaws or imperfections. This is how Jesus' light can work in our lives: It reveals things that are unseen in the darkness or half-light. If we have this light on the throne of our lives, it will reveal what is in our hearts so that we can cut away the dead branches and fruitless activities and grow to become more and more like Jesus every day. This is why people rarely harvest in the dark—it is hard to tell the good fruit from the black and corrupt.

When self is on the throne, our eye is dark through the half-truths we accept to justify our vague lives. *Every half-truth is a whole lie.* We live in the darkness and shadow of self. We don't see things clearly. It is like walking into a room to find your car keys, seeing them on the counter in the shadows, and, upon picking them up, you find instead that you grabbed a tarantula! We are mistaken in the way we see things and are deceived, accepting doctrines and beliefs that are not based on truth. However, since they justify our self-concepts—they appear to be the very thing we are after in the half-light—we embrace them wholeheartedly. Instead of the truth of God, we build our self-images on the foundations of culture, habit, and environment. We haven't the time or inclination to examine things too closely and determine the true nature of those things we accept. Thus, finding ourselves comfortable where we are, we complacently settle for the smallest knowledge of God rather than being constantly hungry for more of Him.

Look again at what Jesus said to the Pharisees:

> You decide according to what you can see and touch. I don't make judgments like that. But even if I did, my judgment would be true because I wouldn't make it out of the narrowness of my experience but in the largeness of the One who sent me, the Father. . . . You're tied down to the mundane; I'm in touch with what is beyond your horizons. You live in terms of what you see and touch. (John 8:15–16, 23 THE MESSAGE)

These religious leaders were deceived because they took the natural world as the sole evidence for the truth; they took the types and shadows as the original. Knowing nothing of the spiritual, they excluded it. Not knowing they had an open door to God if they would only seek Him with all of their hearts, they never knocked on it to be let in. They were quite happy to accept their own little world of friends and culture as all that was needed for life and godliness. In their deficiencies they claimed to be whole, and they shut God out from working in their midst.

Jesus, however, said that even though He lived in the same physical world as they did, experiencing the same things and reading the same Scriptures, His judgment could be counted on as righteous because He didn't judge "out of the narrowness of my experience but in the largeness of the One who sent me, the Father." By becoming one with His Father, Jesus knew the true from the false. He was not limited by what He experienced in the natural because He had experienced the supernatural by spending time with His Father.

This is perhaps also why Jesus said,

> "If any man come to me, and hate not his father, and mother, and wife, and children, and brethren, and sisters, yea, and his own life also, he cannot be my disciple" (Luke 14:26).

Anyone who is not willing to make Jesus the prominent source for truth rather than "Well, my family believes . . ." or "My pastor says . . ." or "I read in a book by such and such minister that . . ." is really not His disciple. Anyone who lives mainly by what another says is not following Jesus; he is following that other person.

I am not saying ministers and books cannot help us come to God, but have you truly examined the nuggets of wisdom you have received from them in the light of Christ and His Word? Or are you simply following something that "sounds good to you" because it feels good to scratch ears that itch for something new? Look at what Paul said about "itching ears":

> For the time will come when men will not put up with sound doctrine. Instead, to suit their own desires, they will gather around them a great number of teachers to say what their itching ears want to hear. They will turn their ears away from the truth and turn aside to myths. (2 Timothy 4:3–4 NIV)

The Preacher's New Anointing

You may remember the children's story *The Emperor's New Clothes*. A con man came to a small kingdom with a vain ruler, posed as a tailor, and made the king a new suit of clothing out of "fabric so fine that only the most refined can see it." Because all those in the palace wanted to get ahead in the royal administration, they didn't have the courage to say that they didn't see the fabric or the suit of clothing. They couldn't admit that they weren't refined—it would be the end of their careers, as they would no longer be accepted and respected by their peers!

So the con-man tailor spun a suit out of nothing and pretended to sew these pieces together to make the king's garment. Then on the great day of presentation, the king decided he would see who in his kingdom was refined and who was not. So he called for a parade. He put on his "new suit" and walked—naked as the day he was born, I believe the expression is—out into the village. For more than three quarters of the route, no one said a word other than *oohs* and *aahs* of admiration—they were all too ashamed to admit that as far as they could tell, the emperor was naked. What would everyone else have thought of them?

This went on, of course, until a small boy, who knew nothing of what was refined or why he should lie, stuck out his finger and shouted, "The emperor has no clothes!" At this point the entire ruse was instantly seen through, and people began to laugh uproariously. The emperor responded by grabbing a coat from someone to cover himself, and stole back to the palace in shame.

The truth had set them all free!

Again, Paul warned Timothy that there would be a time in the church "when people will not listen to the true teaching but will find many more teachers who please them by saying the things they want to hear. They will stop listening to the truth and will begin to follow false stories."[9] Like the emperor in the story above, traveling ministers will parade new messages before congregations—claiming special "anointings" or a unique "touch of God" upon their lives—hoping for big offerings. They teach messages that comfort the fleshly desires of people or make promises of what God will do if they only give offerings large enough to "really show their faith in God." Pastors parade out new programs before their churches, ushering in seeker-friendly messages that neither offend nor convict. Whole denominations proclaim the standards of the Bible as passé and welcome perversion into their midst as "alternative lifestyles" or "other paths to God."

It is time someone stood up and said, "The preacher has no anointing!"

In the latter years of Israel's history, the ark of the covenant was completely empty (originally it held the tablets of the Ten Commandments as a symbol of God's holy law, and the staff of Aaron that had budded as a symbol of God's supernatural power). This emptiness grieved the Spirit of God, but the people continued conducting rituals around it.

In like manner, have fifty-seven million Christians in America today accepted outer religious appearances in place of the real Spirit of God? Like Israel in a bygone era, we say things like "I went to the Ark Sunday"; "I gave toward the Ark"; "I sang in the choir at the Ark." We are affirmed by "the Ark"—the outward appearance of being religious—but have we forgotten what was supposed to be in it?

Israel's reverence was never to be for the ark itself but for what was inside of it. Believers have more revelation of God today than in any previous generation, yet we can't seem to push past our self-concepts into the supernatural power available to us. Within the ark was the Word of God and a symbol of the power of God, but if we are more caught up with outward appearances than having the real goods inside, then we are like white sepulchers—beautiful and clean on the outside, but filled with deadness inside.[10]

> But realize this, that in the last days difficult times will come. For men will be *lovers of self,* lovers of money, boastful, arrogant, revilers, disobedient to parents, ungrateful, unholy, unloving, irreconcilable, malicious gossips, without self-control, brutal, haters of good, treacherous, reckless, conceited, lovers of pleasure rather than lovers of God, *holding to a form of godliness, although they have denied its power;* Avoid such men as these. (2 Timothy 3:1–5 NASB)

Far too many Christians today are more interested in using their Christianity to get what they want out of life than they are in letting Christ use them to reach a hell-bound world. We want a religion that justifies us and makes us feel better about ourselves rather than one that transforms us into the image of Christ.

And those of us who feel that we are the least susceptible to this are perhaps the most vulnerable to its deception. Today the charismatic church is the fastest growing denomination. Christians have joined this movement because they believe that all Jesus did in His ministry is also for today, and yet within those groups are thousands upon thousands experiencing nothing of this power in their own lives. They may shout the loudest, but are they really doing anything else to manifest God's kingdom on the earth?

Just the Plain and Simple Truth

We—the entire body of Christ (especially in the United States)—have become too easily lulled into fleshly complacency, the cause of our spiritual poverty. We are caught up in our accomplishments rather than Christ's ministry. We no longer love truth but only what the truth can do for us. Therefore, when truth is inconvenient, we ignore it. Or, as has become the norm today in business, politics, and the church, we spin the facts to look the way we want them to. Sometimes there is not much difference between "putting things in their best light" and "lying." Those who spin the facts are more interested in appearance than substance.

We want a religion that justifies us and makes us feel better about ourselves rather than one that transforms us into the image of Christ.

Another level of truth is what is actual and factual, plain and simple. What is it that happened or is going on without interpretation or judgment? We know how hard it is to be truly objective in a situation, but those who have been with Jesus should be the most objective people on earth, being able to be honest with themselves, knowing their own faults and shortcomings, and speaking to their own hurt, if necessary, for the sake of the truth.[11]

Perhaps education has been a good example of this. In the past teachers were taught to be firm and uncompromising with students, compelling them to be better and better students. Yet we found this damaging to the students' self-confidence, and it followed suit that poor self-confidence led to poor marks. So in the more recent past, teachers have been taught to be very positive, no matter what the students did, to build their confidence, hoping that eventually this would lead to overall improvement. What, in fact, has happened is that we have a generation of students who now make "confident mistakes" and who, when confronted with them, often scoff at the rebuke.

This type of positive spin is what is happening repeatedly in business. Large corporations, bent on presenting a positive outlook to their shareholders, have gone from "putting things in their best light" to actually misreporting the numbers and lying about the value of their companies. We have seen the same thing in the church, where ministers refuse to admit their human frailties until they reach a point of total meltdown and have to step down from the ministry because of sin or burnout.

The Bible, however, doesn't tell us that either being constantly critical or always looking at things in a positive light is the answer to growing up in Christ. Paul instead advises us:

> That we henceforth be no more children, tossed to and fro, and carried about with every wind of doctrine, by the sleight of men, and cunning craftiness, whereby they lie in wait to deceive; but *speaking the truth in love,* may grow up into him in all things, which is the head, even Christ. (Ephesians 4:14–15)

It is the *truth* that will set us free in every situation, and not the truth as seen through rose-colored glasses. Being positive or critical as a rule is adding judgments and spins to the facts. I believe this is one of the reasons Jesus told us to "judge not."[12] When we add to the truth in any way, shape, or form, we put ourselves in a position to eventually be judged ourselves, just as executives from big businesses are being judged in our courts for their accounting misrepresentations. We need to get back to the basic wisdom of Joe Friday on the TV show *Dragnet:* "Just the facts, ma'am."

Let your statement be, "Yes, yes" or "No, no"; anything beyond these is of evil. (Matthew 5:37 NASB)

Let your yea be yea; and your nay, nay; lest ye fall into condemnation. (James 5:12)

It Is Time to Reprogram

Of the thousands of decisions we make every day, how many do we consciously consider before acting upon them? Chances are, very few. What is more apt to direct our lives is habit. Patterns that we have accepted over time are repeated and justified and become so ingrained in us that we don't even think before we act. *We are trained by what we accept as true, and that training becomes a gut-instinct reaction that directs our every step.* If those things that we have accepted are half-truths, we are stumbling around in the dark more than we are making a difference for the Light.

Such deception rarely goes from point A to point Z in an afternoon. Rarely does a person start in the ministry one day and the next is in bed with someone else's spouse. Rarely does a hard-working employee start a job with the long-range goal of embezzling from it. Who would even consider marrying someone they knew they would murder someday? Though we would never imagine such things at their beginnings, these outcomes happen every day in our society—and in the church. Pastors run off with their secretaries; ushers pocket money from the collection plates; "loving" spouses shoot their mates for some reason or another. "If then the light within you is darkness, how great is that darkness!"[13]

The acceptance of half-truths is like smoking cigarettes. Little by little we take them in, and they darken our insides. After years and years of this, they turn into a dark lump that can't even be penetrated by X-rays. They sap our breath and age us prematurely. Death seeps into us until it kills us, and we are no longer of any use to our families and those that depend on us. Sin, like cancer, grows until it will take over our entire lives. Acceptance of these whole lies sears our consciences to the point that the voice of God can no longer penetrate the black lumps in our hearts.

However, sin is not the whole issue. Just as cancer is one result of taking in smoke from cigarettes, sin is the result of sucking in the half-truths that justify self on the throne. It is flesh carried away by lusts that brings about sin.[14] *Sin is the fruit; flesh is the root.* When we repent of sin, we're dealing with the fruit, which is very important. But cutting out the root, which is self on the throne, is even more important.

Most evangelists, myself included, have preached against the *fruit* of the flesh: drinking, drugs, lying, lust. Great numbers of people go to the altar, give up the "fruit," and two weeks later return to the same altar for the same sins. Repentance must deal with the *root*. If we deal only with pruning the fruit, allowing the tree to live, we only guarantee a bumper crop of fresh sins for the next "revival"!

John the Baptist said that One was coming to lay the axe to the root of the tree.[15] We don't want to merely knock off a little cruelty, unforgiveness, or lying. No matter what we do to the fruit of sin, if we never lay the axe to the root of the flesh, we miss why Jesus came. We must cut off the flesh root (die to self) and graft ourselves into Christ the Vine. *Truth is the axe that will sever the root of selfishness!*

The person of the Holy Spirit gives us the power to see our flesh from an eternal perspective—from the perspective of the sober Truth. Flesh-fed Christians have boasted, "There is therefore no condemnation to them which are in Christ Jesus,"[16] while never realizing that the rest of that Scripture is "who walk not after the flesh, but after the Spirit."[17]

We must absorb ourselves in the truth of God's Word—renewing our minds, as Paul put it.[18] By doing this, habits can be reprogrammed to work in our favor.

> For when for the time ye ought to be teachers, ye have need that one teach you again which be the first principles of the oracles of God; and are become such as have need of milk, and not of strong meat. For every one that useth milk is unskillful in the word of righteousness: for he is a babe. But strong meat belongeth to them that are of full

age, *even those who by reason of use have their senses exercised to discern both good and evil.* (Hebrew 5:12–14)

In other words, if we will feed on God's Word and grow up in Him, there will come a point that we will discern between good and evil and act accordingly without a second thought—this is flesh controlled by the Spirit! This is life with Jesus on the throne of our lives! It is time that we grow up enough to take this meat from the Word and make a lasting difference for His kingdom on earth.

Do You Love Truth More Than Your Own Reputation?

In speaking of the end times and those that would follow false prophets, the Bible tells us:

> They perish because they refused to love the truth and so be saved. (2 Thessalonians 2:10 NIV)

> If we say we have fellowship with Him and yet walk in the darkness, we lie and do not practice the truth. (1 John 1:6 NASB)

Do we love truth? Not the truth that makes us feel good or justifies how we live our lives, but the absolute truth. Those who will risk being one with Jesus will find that His light will reveal much in their lives that is harmful and should be cut off. Yet the good fruit that comes from His Spirit will thrive in this light. Jesus on the throne will shine this light into every nook and cranny and expose everything that needs to be changed or cleaned up. This is exactly what needs to happen if we are to be sanctified—set apart—for His use.

This is not something that will happen overnight, nor is it a place to which we are likely to one day "arrive," where we will be able to sit down and say, "*Now* we are holy." It is a process we go through every day, and the pruning always hurts. But then the opportunities to have Jesus truly work through us to touch other lives makes it all worth it! I can imagine nothing greater than meeting Jesus on that day when I too have finished my race[19] and hear Him say, "Well done, thou good and faithful servant: thou hast been faithful over a few things, I will make thee ruler over many things: enter thou into the joy of thy lord."[20]

It is time to get real with God, soaking ourselves in His light and letting His truth set us free from anything that might keep us from accomplishing His plan for our lives on earth.

CHAPTER SEVEN

Savor the Glory

That they may behold my glory, which thou hast given me.

JOHN 17:24

On the Day of Pentecost, people from many nations were saved, and the foundations of churches were established all over the world through those who were reached in Jerusalem. In less than three hundred years, the Roman Empire, which had ruthlessly persecuted Christians for much of its history, became a Christian empire. In the first centuries, God touched various lives that sought Him—Polycarp in the church at Smyrna, an African named Tertullian, and an Egyptian named Antony. God's power was also seen dramatically, if only occasionally, in the fourth and fifth centuries, as the Italian Jerome translated the Bible into Latin and the Libyan Augustine wrote his classic *Confessions*.

Throughout the Dark Ages, Christian slaves who were shipped to other parts of the world spread the Word of God and revival to their captors. A young slave named Patrick escaped but then returned to his former masters in Ireland with the power of God and transformed the nation with the gospel of Jesus Christ.

In the fourteenth and fifteenth centuries, God's power became more evident again. England's outpouring of the Holy Spirit influenced a young man named John Wycliffe to make the first translation of the Bible from Latin into English. A hundred years later William Tyndale created a new English translation from the original Greek. Around this time, a German named Martin Luther, after seeing corruption in the official church of his day, sparked an entirely different kind of revival when he nailed his famous Ninety-Five Theses to a chapel door in Wittenberg.

The nation of India saw flames of revival in the sixteenth century. In one instance, a minister named Francesco ordered bystanders to open a day-old grave. Francesco fell to his knees, prayed, and commanded the dead man to rise. The man arose to perfect health—and the whole village turned to God.

Even school children have been visited by God. History records three hundred children prophesying in Cevenne, France, at the end of the seventeenth century. The children's revival lasted over a decade until it was forcibly subdued by the French army in 1711.

Moravian exiles saw revival in Germany in 1727 when their regular meeting was disrupted by a burst of God's power and all fifty fell under the power of God. They established a twenty-four-hour prayer chain, which remained unbroken for one hundred years. Their missionaries greatly influenced two ordinary brothers named John and Charles Wesley.

In 1739, God touched the Wesleys and revival spread in Europe. George Whitfield, who fell under the power of God at their meetings, preached the first open-air sermon in England in four hundred years. People cried out or fell under the power of God in his services—something that troubled the twenty-four-year-old evangelist. But a countess wrote to him, "Don't be wiser than God. Let them cry out. It will do a great deal more good than your preaching."

In the meantime, at least fifty thousand people, one-fifth the entire population, were converted in New England between 1737 and 1741, when God used a young evangelist named Jonathan Edwards. This revival touched a young student at Yale College named David Brainerd, who left school for the tribes of the greatly feared Native Americans. God's power that enveloped his meetings was described as "a mighty rushing w

The "Great American Awakening" started
Sunday in 1857 at an Ontario, Canada,
when—without any call for salvation—twer
saved. The church had no full-time minister, ⌐
ognized the "gust of divine power" and launched daily ᴊᴜ
which led to thousands of salvations.

That same year in New York City, Jeremiah Lamphier, an
ordinary businessman led by God, started a noon prayer meeting
near Wall Street. On his first day, four businessmen joined him.
They grew to twenty, then that number doubled. Then the worst
financial panic up to that point in history struck. Banks closed.
Men lost jobs. Families went hungry. Within six months, ten
thousand businessmen gathered for prayer. Twenty other groups
started. At a time when the population of America was only
twenty-six million, an estimated one million people were converted in just two years. It literally shook the nation.

Even while neutralized and unbelieving generations have
waited for the coming of Christ, not realizing He was there with
them all the time, many more of God's children broke through to
be with Jesus in the twentieth century.

John G. Lake was a normal layman who felt the call of God
and pioneered more than five hundred churches in Africa even
though the bubonic plague was decimating the land. His health
astonished doctors, who couldn't understand why he did not
contract the disease himself. At one point, he challenged the phy-
sicians to take some foam from the plague, check it under a
microscope, and then put it on his hand. When they scraped it off
his hand and looked at it under the microscope again, they were
amazed to see that all signs of the disease had died, just as the
apostle Paul once shook off a venomous viper and then went on
about his business.

Such men and women do not try to fulfill their own plans or
visions—they operate in the ministry of Jesus Christ! The spirit of
life in Christ Jesus makes them free from the laws of sin and death.

In 1904 a woman in India formed prayer groups of girls,

ering five hundred strong, who saw prayer answered in July
5 when revival broke out in many Indian cities, including
ombay. Two decades later in China, the Norwegian missionary
Marie Monsen's prayer groups met twice daily for seven years
until revival sprang up. At roughly the same time in Rwanda and
Burundi, East Africa, discouraged missionaries called for a week
of prayer and "humiliation" before God. Within a decade, fifty
thousand people were converted.

After the Second World War, in the outer Hebrides Islands,
off the coast of Scotland, two sisters in their eighties, one blind
and the other arthritic, started praying for revival. They prayed by
name for every person and cottage in their village twice daily.
Unbeknownst to them, seven young men were also praying in a
nearby barn three nights each week. One night after repenting
before God, the young men were knocked onto the floor by the
power of God.

The next day, one of the women told her pastor about a
vision she'd seen the night before of their island's deserted
churches packed with people. He had invited young Duncan
Campbell of Scotland to come over to speak. Duncan spoke un-
eventfully, but after dismissal on the second night, the entire congregation halted outside the church, unable to leave the grounds
because of the power of God. When they returned inside, the
holy presence of God filled the stone building. Within months
the revival encompassed the entire island.

The Glory of God Brings Revival

I deviate from the traditional meaning for "revival" and define
it as "a supernatural visitation within the church and also within
the world." It is a supernatural salvation—a new awakening.

Revival is within us, waiting to be stirred up as on the Day of
Pentecost. Revival is not merely a service, big crowds, enthusiasm,
repentance, or great worship. If we define "revival" as simply a
state of being revived, or quickened, or filled with God's presence,
and not split hairs over the word, we can say that Christ lived on

earth in perpetual revival. He was filled with the presence of th Father. That's why when He saw a widow's grief at the loss of her only son, He reached out and touched the dead boy, who instantly sprang to life.[1] Now that's revival!

Revival is something that happens to believers when we get fed up with being fed up, we get hungry and thirsty for God, and we won't settle for anything but Him. It happens to people whose prayers are like Moses':

> If thy presence go not with me, carry us not up hence. For wherein shall it be known here that I and thy people have found grace in thy sight? is it not in that thou goest with us? so shall we be separated, I and thy people, from all the people that are upon the face of the earth. . . . I beseech thee, show me thy glory. (Exodus 33:15–16, 18)

Moses asked for God's continual presence, and God's glory follows where His presence is welcome.

"Lord, Show Us Your Glory"

The *Westminster Confession* states that the chief end of man is to glorify God and enjoy Him forever. Jesus' sixth unanswered prayer in John 17 was "That they may behold my glory, which thou hast given me."[2] God's glory follows His presence and touches lives. This is true revival. Throughout history His glory has come as individuals have dared to yearn for His presence. As we have just discussed, amazing revival has broken out in areas as a result, but every time they eventually fizzled out. Is this what God has planned for us? Or have we—as the children of Israel did[3]—limited what God really wanted to do?

The destinies of our nations, as well as our individual destinies, are tied up in the destiny of God's purpose: "For whom he foreknew, he also did predestinate to be conformed to the image of His Son."[4] Our destiny is to be like Jesus. Yet even the most sincere attempts to concentrate on a single set of religious goals through willpower and self-discipline leaves the life untouched,

ecome only partially transformed, suffering "moral
hich one part of our nature becomes overfed and
becomes starved. This is trying to live our Chris-
...ity through willpower and the flesh. God's hope for our
futures is quite different.

> And we, who with unveiled faces all reflect the Lord's
> glory, are being transformed into his likeness with ever-
> increasing glory, which comes from the Lord, who is the
> Spirit. (2 Corinthians 3:18 NIV)

We must reflect the glory of the Lord as if we were mirrors
showing His face. *Doxa* is Greek for "glory," meaning "the
weight of impressed forces, the radiance, dazzling, glittering." Our
children reflect us. We reflect books, family, and friends we come
into contact with—as I have said before, we are a product of the
truths we accept—not just momentarily, but they become part of
who we are. We transfer into our innermost being what we reflect
and those we habitually admire.

We cannot change ourselves. Every man's character continues
in its direction until compelled by "impressed forces" to change.
We have failed to put ourselves in the path of such forces.
Through self-dependence, struggles, efforts, and agony, we try to
control ourselves, but only the force of Christ can change us. The
Word of God speaks of clay and a potter.[5] Clay cannot mold itself.
We need the Master Potter to transform us into His design.

Jesus said,

> I have set before thee an open door, and no man can
> shut it, for thou hast a little strength, and hast kept my
> word, and hast not denied my name. (Revelation 3:8)

Jesus showed us that one way to open that door is to have
little confidence in our own strength. We live in a generation that
loves to boast about how much power we have. Christ always
works through those who recognize how much power *He* has.

The men who became disciples were raw, unspiritual, unin-
spired men. But the Bible says these ordinary, unschooled men

astonished everyone because they had been with Jesus.[6] Being with Jesus changes us from "glory to glory."[7] Paul was absorbed in Christ. When we dwell intently in the Highest, we reflect the Highest.

> [I am] confident of this very thing, that He which hath begun a good work in you will perform [perfect] it until the day of Jesus Christ. (Philippians 1:6)

When we try to repair our damaged sense of identity or heal the wounds of our own hearts, we get ahead of the first order of business and risk putting ourselves in the center of our universe. Self-interest becomes the dominant concern. Flesh always resists even the slightest demands of the spirit. Christ will be reflected in us with all His glory when we have dealt with our stubborn commitment to self-centeredness.

The pathway to revival is clearly marked. It always starts by admitting we are not yet where we need to be with God and then building the desire within ourselves to conform closer to the image of what God has called us to be. It is one thing to be willing to say a prayer, but it is another to become a living prayer. It is one thing to make a sacrifice, but it is another to become a living sacrifice. We too often believe we can make a "small sacrifice" for Jesus—thinking that is enough—rather than obeying and being a "whole sacrifice" by placing control of our lives on the altar of God.

Flesh always resists even the slightest demands of the spirit.

> Therefore I urge you, brethren, by the mercies of God, to present your bodies a living and holy sacrifice, acceptable to God, which is your spiritual service of worship. (Romans 12:1 NASB)

Christians today tend to use the phrase "God is moving." Yet you won't read the apostle Paul telling people the Holy Spirit was moving. He just moved. I'm afraid that sometimes when people emphasize the Holy Spirit's moving, He is moving right out of the place, because the attention is not on the Holy Spirit, it is on the flesh. Today we have so little Spirit power that we spend an enormous amount of time witnessing to each other rather than allowing the Holy Spirit to bear witness to Jesus.

Pastor David Yongii Cho once said to another pastor, who has since passed away, "You're a Holy Ghost atomic bomb." The pastor became very excited.

"Really?" he said. "Has God showed you anything else about my ministry?"

"Yes," Dr. Cho said. "He showed me you're trying to blow up a piggy bank!"

Here we are, the stewards of the greatest power on earth, great enough to create an entire universe from nothing, yet what are we doing with it? Are we using it to try to get into other people's money? Why seek pennies when you can have eternal change? *God's power isn't to be used to take but to give.*

God Has Bigger Plans

Evangelist David Wilkerson, a friend for many years, said to me as he commented on a great revival, "This is not that."[8] He was not diminishing the power of the revival. He was saying, "Before there can be a great awakening that shakes America, there has to be a rude awakening. That's what's coming next." The shaking of cities and entire nations! Things that have happened in Toronto, Pensacola, and elsewhere are just the first-fruits, but we're going *beyond*!

God has decreed an end-time manifestation of His power and glory that will shake the world and take us beyond Pentecost, beyond mere revivals. He will take us beyond these because He will take us beyond ourselves.

We want what we've been promised—the present-day ministry of Jesus operating within us *unhindered.*

It is time we each see such a move of God in our lives! Christians today comprise thirty-three percent of the total world population, over two billion strong, yet the minutest fraction of us have experienced the present-day ministry of Christ unhindered. Think of what will happen when we all do!

When great saints pray, they stir up a flame of the Spirit within themselves. Instead of praying, "God, send revival," they all discover the same thing: The person of Jesus Christ revealed by the Holy Spirit *is* revival. We need to stand up at His command and declare His presence. God's glory! It's all about Jesus! When we are ultimately acquainted with Jesus, we are drawn into the presence of the Father that leads to His glory!

I was at a church outside of New Orleans many years ago when, even before I preached, Jesus softly said, "Stand up and declare a spirit of salvation." *How odd,* I thought. But I obeyed and said what Jesus told me to.

When you say what Jesus says, you will see what Jesus sees and you will do what Jesus does.

Instantly, when I spoke Christ's words, the power of God hit that building. The large chandelier started shaking, then the whole building shook. I was told that the pastor's wife called the police to find out if there was an earthquake. There was not, but sixty-two people who did not know Christ jumped out of their seats and rushed to the altar for salvation.

The visitation of God's glory is heaven-sent revival. A heaven-sent revival is Holy Spirit power within us manifesting the present-day ministry of Jesus Christ. *All we need are hearts hungry enough to believe His Word and act upon it in His wisdom.*

The church in the book of Acts caused demons to tremble. Christians roared with fire and glory. There was nothing they wouldn't do for the honor of God. There were no territorial rights, no spirit of competition, no power plays, no arrogance, and no big egos.

The great teacher E. M. Bounds said, "Programs, techniques, campaigns are utterly useless unless people are under the control of the Holy Spirit. Men are God's methods. While men look for better methods, God looks for better men." We can be those for whom God is looking!

Don't Tell Me How Revival Started, Tell Me Why It Stopped

Perhaps the greatest question for us today is not how revival starts, but what kills it? It is hard to believe that God would reach out to His people, touch them briefly, then intentionally retreat to leave them stranded. Before Jesus returns, the Gospel will have to spread in at least one last world revival. Will we be part of that or a hindrance to it?

> *Perhaps the greatest question for us today is not how revival starts, but what kills it?*

To the apostle Paul, his fleshly self was not a mere setback, not a drama or a hurdle to be overcome. To Paul it was a fatal wound, a deadly disease.

I used to think I should be horrified by my flesh, that I should control it, squelch the evil out, and discipline myself unto righteousness. But Paul went far beyond that, saying he was never surprised at what his flesh was capable of, because in his flesh dwelled "no good thing."[9] We need not expect ourselves to be better than we are. We must allow the transcendent life of Christ to carry us beyond our flesh. What we cannot control, Christ can transcend.

When we're squeezed, what's inside is going to come out. Because darkness is increasing as we move toward the end of the age, pressure will increase upon every believer. The flesh has to be dealt with so that only the Spirit of God comes out of us.

> The people that do know their God will be strong, and do exploits. (Daniel 11:32)

This prophecy will be fulfilled through those of us willing to pay the price.

We cannot live until we learn how to die. This is the greatest paradox in history. The Israelites were given only one use for animal flesh—to burn it.[10] Every day priests robed in the attire of righteousness carried the flesh outside the camp and arranged the burnt offering carefully to ensure no flesh would escape the flames. They constantly added more to fuel the fire. Revival today is the fire of God, sent so we can die to our flesh and become alive to His Spirit.

Why hasn't the repentance message changed this nation? It's been preached since the founding of America by some of the greatest orators and ministers, with sweeping revivals following. But the spirit behind each movement died because people repented for sinful deeds—the fruit of our flesh, not the root of it—then left, thinking they were holy. The battle is not sin against righteousness but flesh against spirit.

The Word of God calls us "children of wrath"[11] when we fulfill the desires of the flesh. We wrestle against our own flesh and never enter the real fight, which is against principalities, powers, rulers of darkness, and spiritual wickedness in high places.[12] No wonder Paul said he wanted to be delivered from this "body of death."

In the Roman Empire during Paul's time, one punishment for murder was that the murderer would be chained to the dead body of his victim. The murderer would live with that decaying corpse until the dead body killed the living body. Paul understood that his dead and decaying flesh was a killer to his spirit in much the same way.

Flesh Has Squelched All the Revivals!

The flesh loses its hold as we live in Christ. This is the difference between religion and life.

> Walk in the Spirit, and ye shall not fulfill the lust of the flesh. (Galatians 5:16)

What kills revivals? Religious flesh. Manipulating flesh, competing flesh, angry flesh, jealous flesh, covetous flesh, and controlling flesh. Flesh creates kingdoms even in churches—in fact, as many kingdoms, if not more, than are outside of the church.

Once we've truly known Christ, human religion will never

satisfy us again. We'll cry out, "There has to be more!"

As the priests of old, we must daily ensure every scrap of the flesh—all its works, all its lusts, all its ego—is burned. Then our fire of revival can blaze. *We have never yet put enough flesh on the fire to keep revival flames burning!*

Religious flesh stands at the door of the Holy of Holies with hands folded, smugly believing we have been with Jesus in our quiet time—but blocking the entrance to the glory of God.

Leonard Ravenhill stated, "A man that has been with Jesus will never fear man." The fact that most of us live to please others before God testifies against us, and yet we wonder why demons do not tremble and our prayers do not get answered. As long as we make people our primary preoccupation, pleasing them and ourselves, we will be disqualified from going beyond hit-and-miss "revivals" to the greatest awakening the world will ever see.

The world is waiting to see God's Spirit on us like a royal insignia pressed into the wax of a sealed document.[13]

We can't convince a lost and dying world to embrace the Good News until we deal with the bad news—that we, God's people who have been called by His name, have not humbled ourselves. We have not sought His face. We have not repented from our wicked ways.[14]

Yet God is raising up a people who are determined to be of no personal reputation so that Christ might be all in all, Lord of Lords, and King of Kings. God is raising up a people who are hungry and thirsty to give up the low life of being people pleasers to gain the life of Christ.

A lost and dying world will cry out after what we have when they see we have been with Jesus—not by what we say, but by the glory of God that is manifested through our private and public lives. The heavens will open when the flesh surrenders to the present-day ministry of Jesus Christ, allowing it to rule and reign. If anything can make us despise our sinful flesh, it is the true revelation of the price Christ paid at the Cross.

If the Christian life can be lived in the flesh, then Jesus died in vain.

Being with Jesus is for those who will pursue His presence, and *His private presence has always come before His public power.* D. L. Moody said it this way: "Let us remove all hindrances to revival that come from ourselves. Revival must begin with us."

Every time the world has seen a glimpse of Jesus from one of the great revivalists, people have responded with repentance. Imagine what would happen if the world would see the life of Jesus in millions of Christians whose fires burn brightly every day. Satan fears the body of Christ learning to love the smell of burning flesh through the fire of the Holy Spirit, because it will release the glory of God like the world has never seen. It is that glory that will have to come before Jesus can return. God is waiting on us to wait upon Him.

CHAPTER EIGHT

Are You Perfect? Why Not?

That they may be made perfect in one.

JOHN 17:23

In 1991 I had over eight hours of surgery on my neck. I was in pain, depressed, broken, and terribly worried about whether I would ever preach again. But as I lay in bed, only a week and a half after surgery, Jesus spoke to my heart to go to the Middle East. Operation Desert Storm had started, and Jesus was sending me from a surgical ward to a war zone. One of the places God sent me to on that trip was Iraq, where I preached in a field to refugees day and night for a week until what strength I did have was gone and my voice ached with hoarseness. I didn't realize that in my weakened condition, I was in perfect position for a "kiss of God."

For my last sermon, I heard Jesus softly speaking to preach on Jonah and Nineveh. I preached it the best I could, how when Jonah finally went there, the king of Nineveh repented and a great revival broke out, yet Jonah was disappointed. I was also disappointed, because when I challenged the people to come forward and accept Christ, only one old man came. My interpreter said, "Why aren't you rejoicing?"

"I'm happy for one soul," I said, "but I was hoping for more."

"My dear brother," the interpreter said, "the one soul who just found Jesus is the current king of Nineveh! He is the Kurdish sheik of sixteen provinces, and the capital is the site of ancient Nineveh. He has accepted Jesus and has invited you to go to Nineveh because he believes if you will preach, they will repent."

Despite my inadequacies and flaws, it turned out I was the perfect person in the perfect place to manifest God's kingdom. In my yieldedness, God made up for my weaknesses with His strength and I was "perfect" for the job at hand.

The Perfect Solution

Jesus' seventh unanswered prayer in John 17 was "That they may be made perfect in one."[1] Much too often we define "perfect" as "without flaw or defect; unblemished and pure, lacking nothing." We say, "Oh, I'm not perfect and never will be. Jesus was the only perfect person who ever walked the earth." Or we think of the end products of an assembly line, each individual item rolling down a conveyer belt looking exactly like the one before it, ad infinitum. In these cases, each product's "perfection" is measured by how closely it fits the one original design.

In this sense and using this definition only, it is true that none of us is perfect. Certainly none of us is without flaw or defect, not lacking anything, or matching some one standard of "perfect" to which we were all originally supposed to conform. But the definitions of "perfect" in the Bible are somewhat different. It is important to understand what "perfect" means in the Bible to truly understand what Jesus was praying for us.

In the Old Testament, the word *perfect* is translated from the Hebrew word *tamiym,* meaning "complete, whole, entire, sound . . . healthful . . . wholesome, unimpaired, innocent, having integrity . . . what is complete or entirely in accord with truth and fact."[2] It is the word used to describe the condition of a lamb that would be sacrificed for a sin offering. If a sheep can be considered perfect, then why can't a person? *This perfection is not related to the absence of character faults but the fitness of the thing for the task at hand.*

The word *perfect* in John 17:23 is the Greek word *teleioō*, which means "(1) to carry through completely, to accomplish, finish, bring to an end. . . . (2) [to] add what is yet wanting in order to render a thing full. . . . (3) to bring to the end (goal) proposed. (4) to accomplish."[3] A slightly different derivative of this root word is defined as "(1) brought to its end, finished. (2) wanting nothing necessary to completeness. . . . (4) full grown, adult, of full age, mature."[4]

Another word translated as "perfect" in the Scriptures is *katartisis*, which means "a making fit . . . implying a process leading to consummation."[5] In other words, in the Scriptures, "perfect" has more of a meaning of being "fit for" or accomplishing something, as in the fulfillment of prophecy. This is one aspect of how Jesus was perfect—He was the perfect sacrifice to perfect the promise of the law; He is the Alpha and Omega, the beginning and the end. In this sense, we can be perfect as well, when we fit ourselves into God's plan to help manifest God's will for someone at a certain time.

In this light, it is easy to see that a totally "imperfect" (modern meaning) vessel or tool can be "perfect" (Bible meaning) for a given task. A plug with a nick in it may be the perfect fit for a hole that has a rough edge in it. We would say they fit together *perfectly* even though both parts are not perfect in themselves.

It may also be that we design something, say a tool, that is unique, a serious deviation from the original design for that tool, so that it can accomplish a very special task. Though it is imperfect with respect to the design of the original, it is perfect for the peculiar task. A good example would be a tool that has been re-designed for a man that has lost a finger so that it will fit perfectly into his hand.

At the age of thirty-one, I faced the greatest crisis of my life. I had been working eighteen hours a day, seven days a week, trying to be the best I could be. I had no comprehension that I was competing—competing for acceptance among my peers. I was addicted to work in the same way an alcoholic is addicted to alcohol or a drug addict is addicted to drugs. That addiction began to break my health.

An undiagnosed neurological disease began to manifest itself. It caused all the muscles in my neck to spasm. I began to experience panic attacks and tachycardia. My heart rate would jump from 80 to 200 beats in a matter of seconds.

As a result, I ended up in the cardiology ward. *Why?* I kept asking God. I wept for over fourteen months, sitting on the back steps of our ministry offices, crying—all the emotions of the pain and hurt I had experienced as a child resurfacing. Instead of seeing the faces of those around me, the only face I could see was my father's—laughing, and telling me what a failure I was. I knew I was failing, even dying. What I didn't realize was that I *had* to die—die to my flesh and my pride. I'd lived the Christian life but not the Christ-life.

In the midst of my darkness, I became depressed, discouraged, and physically weak. I cried out to God from that cardiology ward, "Lord, I've never wanted to know you in the fellowship of your suffering, but I do now." As I said that, the Lord said, "Then you shall know me in the power of my resurrection. Because you are willing to admit what you are not, I will empower you with what I am. Where those two points meet, destiny will be birthed in your life." Little did I know that several months later the soft, gentle voice of the Holy Spirit would speak to me to read:

> Remember ye not the former things, neither consider the things of old. Behold *I will do a new thing*; now it shall spring forth; shall ye not know it; I will even make a way in the wilderness, and rivers in the desert. (Isaiah 43:18–19)

Through this Scripture a drop of water fell on my parched spirit. Next I heard Jesus softly say to go home, send a fax to Israeli Prime Minister Menachem Begin, and he would meet with me. I argued, "No, Lord, there's no way. He doesn't even like me, so why would he want to see me?"

Finally I obeyed His voice and sent the fax telling Prime Minister Begin I'd be in a Jerusalem hotel for six days and desired to meet with him. I flew there, checked in, and went to prayer.

On my second day, I found myself in the prime minister's office. I started with, "Hello, how are you?" and then he talked for almost thirty minutes, which was good because I had nothing to say.

Finally he asked, "Why did you come?"

"I don't know why I came."

"You don't know?" he said with astonishment. "What do you know?"

"God sent me," I said.

"God sent you but didn't tell you why?" he asked, becoming amused at the situation.

"No, He didn't tell me why," I said, somewhat embarrassed.

He called for his secretary to come into his office.

"Eight thousand miles, Kadashai, to meet with me, and he says nothing except God sent him. Kadashai, shake his hand. We have finally found an honest man!"

Then he turned to me and asked, "When God tells you why, will you come back and tell me?"

After leaving the prime minister's office I still didn't know why I'd gone, so I prayed and waited for an answer. Finally Jesus softly spoke one word to me: "bridge." Once I had that, I called him and met with him again.

As before, after our introductions, he asked, "Why did you come?"

I only had the one word, so I said, "To build a bridge."

"A bridge? Like the Brooklyn Bridge?" the prime minister prodded. "What kind of bridge?"

I had no idea what to say, but as I opened my mouth, out popped, "A bridge of love." Immediately Jesus' gentle voice became clear on the inside of me as to what He intended for my life through this meeting.

"A bridge of love," he mused. "I like that—for whom?"

"Between Christians in America and Jews in Israel," I answered.

"I like that," Begin said again. "I will help you."

That was the start of a twenty-year, Jesus-blessed relationship with the nation of Israel that revolutionized my life as the bridge Jesus wanted to build became a reality.

By not caring about my reputation, God was able to use me. Somehow I fit perfectly into His plan, allowing my imperfections to draw me closer to God rather than make me more distant from Him.

Defining "Perfect" God's Way

Jesus' prayer was that we would be "perfect in one," or, you could say, "complete in unity." In this sense we see that perfection can never be realized without the rest of the body of Christ. Just as an orchestra trying to operate without violins or without a percussion section is imperfect in the sense of being incomplete, so we in the body of Christ are imperfect when we are not working together as God designed us to. Each individual part has to do what it is supposed to do, just as each individual part of an engine must function correctly and in union with the others for the motor to provide enough power to make a car move. Paul said it this way:

> He [God] . . . gave some, apostles; and some, prophets; and some, evangelists; and some, pastors and teachers; *For the perfecting of the saints,* for the work of the ministry, for the edifying of the body of Christ: Till we all come in the unity of the faith, and of the knowledge of the Son of God, *unto a perfect man, unto the measure of the stature of the fulness of Christ:* That we henceforth be no more children, tossed to and fro, and carried about with every wind of doctrine, by the sleight of men, and cunning craftiness, whereby they lie in wait to deceive; But speaking the truth in love, may grow up into him in all things, which is the head, even Christ: *From whom the whole body fitly joined together and compacted by that which every joint supplieth, according to the effectual working in the measure of every part, maketh increase of the body unto the edifying of itself in love.* (Ephesians 4:11–16)

By finding our unique destiny and function within His body, we become part of that perfecting of His work—fitting perfectly into His plan for manifesting His kingdom on the earth. It is time we stopped saying, "What do you expect? Nobody's perfect!" and start becoming perfect through the knowledge, presence, and wisdom of God. After all, we are commanded to be perfect again and again in His Word. Would God command us to do something that He knew we could never attain?

> The LORD appeared to Abram, and said unto him, "I am the Almighty God; walk before me, and *be thou perfect*" (Genesis 17:1).
>
> Thou shalt *be perfect* with the LORD thy God. (Deuteronomy 18:13)
>
> Let your heart therefore *be perfect* with the LORD our God, to walk in his statutes, and to keep his commandments, as at this day. (1 Kings 8:61)
>
> *Be ye therefore perfect,* even as your Father which is in heaven is perfect. (Matthew 5:48)
>
> "If thou wilt enter into life, keep the commandments."
>
> He saith unto him, "Which?"
>
> Jesus said, "Thou shalt do no murder, Thou shalt not commit adultery, Thou shalt not steal, Thou shalt not bear false witness, Honor thy father and thy mother: and, Thou shalt love thy neighbor as thyself."
>
> The young man saith unto him, "All these things have I kept from my youth up: what lack I yet?"
>
> Jesus said unto him, "*If thou wilt be perfect,* go and sell that thou hast, and give to the poor, and thou shalt have treasure in heaven: and come and follow me" (Matthew 19:17–21).
>
> The disciple is not above his master: but *every one that is perfect* shall be as his master. (Luke 6:40)
>
> Finally, brethren, farewell. *Be perfect,* be of good comfort, be of one mind, live in peace; and the God of love and peace shall be with you. (2 Corinthians 13:11)

How is it that we have so easily passed perfection off as unattainable? What have convention and culture robbed from the church for us to think perfection is outside of our grasp? If God has commanded us to be perfect, then did He command us to do something that we can never hope to accomplish? Or is there some misunderstanding of the term that is shutting us out from the "enabling" that God is trying to get to us?

Growing in Perfection

If we also think that perfection is one point to "arrive at" and that "once perfect" that is enough, look at what Paul had to say about it to the Philippians:

> Brethren, I count not myself to have apprehended: but this one thing I do, forgetting those things which are behind, and reaching forth unto those things which are before, I press toward the mark for the prize of the high calling of God in Christ Jesus.
> Let us therefore, as many as *be perfect,* be thus minded. (Philippians 3:13–15)

Obviously, we need to change our thinking in a few areas.

Here is another opportunity for us to dump our conventional thinking and come into agreement with Jesus' prayer. If we are commanded to be perfect and Jesus prayed that we would be perfect, then *we must be able to be perfect.*

The simplest way I can think of to define this perfection we are called to, in the biblical sense, is "being in the right place, at the right time, knowing the will of God, and being ready to perform it."

At our first crusade in India, the Holy Spirit told me we would see the greatest harvest of souls ever. I'd never been to India, no one knew me, and my flesh was saying, "They don't know you, they don't know your reputation, no one will show up." To this Jesus softly replied, "Be grateful, it's a blessing; therefore, the only reputation they will know of is Mine."

The night before the crusade began, I had a vision. I saw the throne room of God and Jesus. Next to them were hundreds of idols. Jesus asked, "Whose idols are these?" I was going to say, "They're the idols of India," but I stopped when I saw the names on them. Jesus had revealed my own idols to me. When I awoke, my pillow was a sponge of tears. I fell like a dead man on my hands and knees, and I crawled into the next room.

My teenage daughter, Shira, joined me in weeping, and soon we were joined by our entire crusade team. All night we travailed in emptying ourselves of our selves before the Lord.

> *The night before the crusade began, I had a vision. I saw the throne room of God and Jesus. Next to them were hundreds of idols.*

I felt like the most unqualified man in the world to preach the next day, yet more than 250,000 Muslims and Hindus came to Christ that week! People flew in from all over the nation and lined up in front of my hotel room door, all the way down to the street, wanting me to pray for them. Even a government leader came with his aide, wanting prayer. Jesus had showed up in His glory.

What I had called "imperfect," Jesus said was "perfect" for the job at hand. I had to change the way I saw things.

Paul's attitude was that he was already perfect—fit and ready to do the will of God in any place at any time—but at the same time he was striving for more of God, a more intimate relationship with Jesus, and a greater influence of the Holy Spirit in his life. He was pressing "toward the mark for the prize of the high calling of God in Christ Jesus." *Today's English Version* paraphrases this as "God's call through Christ Jesus to the life above."[6] Look at how *The Message* puts this passage:

> Friends, don't get me wrong: By no means do I count myself an expert in all of this, but I've got my eye on the goal, where God is beckoning us onward—to Jesus. I'm off and running, and I'm not turning back.
>
> So let's keep focused on that goal, *those of us who want everything God has for us.* If any of you have something else in mind, something less than total commitment, God will

clear your blurred vision—you'll see it yet! Now that we're on the right track, let's stay on it.

Stick with me, friends. Keep track of those you see running this same course, headed for this same goal. There are many out there taking other paths, choosing other goals, and trying to get you to go along with them. I've warned you of them many times; sadly, I'm having to do it again. All they want is easy street. They hate Christ's Cross. But easy street is a dead-end street. Those who live there make their bellies their gods; belches are their praise; all they can think of is their appetites.

But there's far more to life for us. (Philippians 3:13–20)

Here the line "as many as be perfect" is rendered "those of us who want everything God has for us." Does this sound like those committed to manifesting God's kingdom on the earth? Does it sound like you?

Are You Ready?

We have already talked a good deal about getting to truly know Jesus; becoming one with Him, His purposes, and His present-day ministry; and other things we need to do to know His will and how to obey it, but are we *ready* to perform it? Are we ready to do the "greater works" Jesus said believers would do? What exactly do we need to do to be ready to do these good works of God?

One thing the Scriptures tell us about this is in Paul's advice to Timothy:

Be diligent to present yourself approved to God as a workman who does not need to be ashamed, accurately handling the word of truth. . . .

Now in a large house there are not only gold and silver vessels, but also vessels of wood and of earthenware, and some to honor and some to dishonor. Therefore, if anyone cleanses himself from these things, he will be a vessel for honor, sanctified, useful to the Master, *prepared for every good work.*

Now flee from youthful lusts and pursue righteousness, faith, love and peace, with those who call on the Lord from a pure heart. . . .

All Scripture is inspired by God and profitable for teaching, for reproof, for correction, for training in righteousness; so that the man of God may be adequate [the King James Version says "perfect"], *equipped for every good work.* (2 Timothy 2:15, 20–22; 3:16–17 NASB)

A big part of being ready to do the will of God at all times is being thoroughly grounded in the Word of God—no, not what others have taught you about it, not what your church says about it or what you have read about it in commentaries or other books (these were, after all, the errors of religious leaders in Jesus' day), but *what the Word of God says to you plainly and simply.* Yes, it is possible that you may need to work some of it out with other believers and ministers to mine out the truth and separate that truth from the errors caused by our own human thinking and misunderstandings—but, after all, a big part of our "perfection" is working in community with other members of the body of Christ.

> *A big part of being ready to do the will of God at all times is being thoroughly grounded in the Word of God.*

The question is not whether or not you have yet attained, but are you in pursuit? It is the strangest thing, but truth seems to exist more in the pursuit of it than in the realization—more in the journey than in the arrival. Somehow the person who thinks he has reached the highest truths is the farthest from them, but those who are the hungriest and most desperate for them seem the closest. There is something in our openness to seeking the truth—the whole truth and nothing but the truth—that allows God to speak it to us more clearly, while there is something in the thought that we have already achieved "truth" that deafens us to His voice as He tries to reach us with the revelation that we need.

Whether this is because we fall into pride, scald our consciences, or simply begin to walk in deception, I don't know. All I do know is that at the moment I set down the pick and stop digging with all my might for the gold of God's truth and presence—start thinking "I have finally arrived"—I am led to a despairing moment when I realize I was much further from God than I thought I was. My only solution to this has been to continue to seek Him with all my heart at all times—to stay thirsty for His presence and hungry to do His will. Anything less is to let self slip stealthily back to the throne of my life and head me toward a new shipwreck.

For example, if we take the idea that we can be perfect—that we are truly perfect in Christ—as a new revelation and a point of attainment, then we might begin by changing the way we speak and say to ourselves, "I *am* perfect through what Jesus has done for me at the Cross!" There is nothing wrong with this. In fact, we *should* change the way we speak, for our mouths speak what fills our hearts.[7] If we have this revelation truly planted in our hearts, then that is what should come out! If you still find yourself saying casually, "Well, no one's perfect!" then you need to look at what the Bible says about perfection again, because your mouth is telling you that you still believe something else.

The problem is that it is very easy for us to stop at the point of changing the way we speak without truly letting it change the way we live. We never seem as interested in living "the life above" as we are in looking good before others. It is too easy to get caught up with making sure we always say the right thing and know the right doctrine. This, then, just becomes another list of manmade rules. It is simply another way of giving lip service to God while self sits more and more securely on the throne of our hearts![8]

This is why Jesus so adamantly warned us not to judge teachers that come to us by the accuracy of their doctrines and what they say but by the fruit that comes out of their lives and ministries:

Beware of false prophets, which come to you in sheep's clothing, but inwardly they are ravening wolves. *Ye shall know them by their fruits.* Do men gather grapes of thorns, or figs of thistles? Even so every good tree bringeth forth good fruit; but a corrupt tree bringeth forth evil fruit. A good tree cannot bring forth evil fruit, neither can a corrupt tree bring forth good fruit. Every tree that bringeth not forth good fruit is hewn down, and cast into the fire. Wherefore by their fruits ye shall know them.

Not every one that saith unto me, "Lord, Lord," shall enter into the kingdom of heaven; but he that doeth the will of my Father which is in heaven. Many will say to me in that day, "Lord, Lord, have we not prophesied in thy name? and in thy name have cast out devils? and in thy name done many wonderful works?" And then will I profess unto them, "I never knew you: depart from me, ye that work iniquity." *Therefore whosoever heareth these sayings of mine, and doeth them, I will liken him unto a wise man, which built his house upon a rock: And the rain descended, and the floods came, and the winds blew, and beat upon that house; and it fell not: for it was founded upon a rock.* And every one that heareth these sayings of mine, and doeth them not, shall be likened unto a foolish man, which built his house upon the sand: And the rain descended, and the floods came, and the winds blew, and beat upon that house; and it fell: and great was the fall of it. (Matthew 7:15–27)

Do you see what Jesus is saying here? Someone may be sitting right next to you in the pew, saying the same thing and singing the same songs, but his heart is far from God! (Look at the parable of the wheat and the tares—Matthew 13:24–30—for another example of this.) The fruit in his life is the only way you can tell where his heart really is, not what comes out of his mouth. He may even appear to do the works of God and operate in the gifts of the Holy Spirit, but in truth, the way he lives day to day in private and away from the crowds has a great deal more to do with selfishness than godliness. When push comes to shove, his decisions will be based on what is best for himself, ignoring the dictates of God's love and His Word, while with his mouth he speaks out Bible phrases and "faith" to justify his actions. More often than not, he has even deceived himself, and only the presence of the Holy Spirit will ever bring him back to the truth.[9]

Therefore, don't fall into the trap of feeling that you are somehow unique now that you can say, "I am perfect," while the rest of the body of Christ is still blind to this biblical fact. The fact is, you were special to God before you learned this and you are just as special afterward! Nor should you take it upon yourself to correct the rest of the body when they say, "Nobody's perfect!" What you should do is keep your mouth shut and *take it upon yourself to live it!*

Just as binding ourselves with His Word and His revelation becomes a threefold cord that is not easily broken, so is aligning what we say with what we believe and *what we do*. Our words and beliefs are meaningless without our actions. As James said, "Faith without works is dead."[10] That is why we see the lives and ministries of too many unraveling before our eyes—they are now eating the product of the bitter fruit they have sown for so long because they have continued to preach and teach one thing and live another. You can say Christ is on the throne of your life as much as you want, but if you don't obey Him and His Word when it is plainly before you, then it is self you are in submission to, not Jesus.

When you are hidden in Christ, Satan can only see Jesus. It is not your righteousness but Christ's that is manifested. Our concern is not to "be perfect" or "be righteous" but to be *in Christ*.

Be Like Micah

I hope I haven't made this sound complicated, because it really isn't. We just have to be honest and be like Micah:

> What can we bring to the LORD to make up for what we've done? Should we bow before God with offerings of yearling calves? Should we offer him thousands of rams and tens of thousands of rivers of olive oil? Would that please

the LORD? Should we sacrifice our firstborn children to pay for the sins of our souls? Would that make him glad?

No, O people, the LORD has already told you what is good, and this is what he requires: *to do what is right, to love mercy, and to walk humbly with your God.* (Micah 6:6–8 NLT)

Do right, love mercy, and walk humbly with God day by day. If we do this, constantly seeking His whole truth to meet the needs of each day and being ready at all times to obey His voice and His Word, then the rest will take care of itself. And that *rest* is the wildest, most joyful ride you could ever hope to take! It is "living the life above on the earth below." Do this, and the God on the inside of you will become so real that His presence in you will change the world around you!

It is time we became answers to Jesus' prayers. Are you ready to do His will?

CHAPTER NINE

Living Epistles

That the world may know that thou hast sent me, and hast loved them, as thou hast loved me.

JOHN 17:23

Now they saw the boldness of Peter and John, and perceived that they were unlearned and ignorant men, they marvelled; and they took knowledge of them, *that they had been with Jesus*.

ACTS 4:13

Have you been with Jesus?

Another great element of "being perfect"—"a vessel fit for the Master's use"—is *time*. As human beings, we tend to spend most of our time preoccupied with what we value most. Just as a young person in love spends a great deal of time thinking of his significant other, and fathers or mothers with demanding jobs tend to be unavailable at home when their minds are always at the office, most of us tend to obsess over the things that we think give our lives the most meaning and value.

In this way, young Christians seem obsessed with witnessing and learning everything they can about God because of the profound redefining impact being born again has upon their lives. Yet this first love too often turns to complacency as we let other things come into our lives and crowd out our time with Jesus.[1]

Somehow faith turns to mental assent, passion turns to tolerance, and we learn "Christianese" as a way of pleasing people, with little concern for what heaven thinks about how we live out our daily lives. On the outside, we live to gain the acceptance of others, whether they believe in God or not, while in our hearts, self and its desires become more and more firmly enthroned.

It is one thing to know something intellectually but quite another to be able to live it out on a regular basis, just as knowing the correct golf or tennis swing intellectually rarely means that we play perfectly on the course or court. The only way to make the transfer from brain to performance is to *spend time practicing what we know to the point that it becomes natural.* In the military, soldiers practice readiness and learn to perform defense techniques that they may never use or only use once in their entire lives. Paul likened us to such soldiers.[2] We need to put into practice the principles of God's Word to the point that we hear and obey His voice so naturally that when the greater works require doing, we are available to God to be used for His glory.

Just as the book of Hebrews tells us we can get into the milk and meat of the Word to the point that even our physical senses— our internal, subconscious programming, if you will—can tell the difference between good and evil,[3] we need to walk with Jesus on such a consistent basis that His voice is always clear to us and we are ever ready to perform His will. Just as Moses had to cover his face because it glowed with God's presence,[4] God's presence should go with us to the point that the world takes notice. This comes from spending time with Jesus. It was with this thought in mind that Paul called the believers in Corinth "living letters" written about the goodness of God as a spiritual testimony of Jesus wherever they went:

> You are our letter, written in our hearts, *known and read by all men*; being manifested that *you are a letter of Christ,* cared for by us, *written not with ink but with the Spirit of the living God,* not on tablets of stone but on tablets of human hearts. (2 Corinthians 3:2–3 NASB)

Have you been with Jesus?

Becoming the Walking Will of God

Jesus' eighth unanswered prayer in John 17 was, "Then the world will know that you sent me and will understand that you love them as much as you love me."[5] How can the world know how much God loves us unless His love becomes outwardly evident in our lives? When is the last time someone *accused* you of being a Christian?

When Peter entered the courtyard of the palace the night Jesus was being tried for His life, he was accused of having been with Jesus. In response, he denied it. He was accused three times, and he denied it three times. He was afraid that "having been with Jesus" would cost him his life. He couldn't have been more correct. Being with Jesus will cost you everything.

> If any of you wants to be my follower . . . you must put aside your selfish ambition, shoulder your cross, and follow me. If you try to keep your life for yourself, you will lose it. But if you give up your life for my sake and for the sake of the Good News, you will find true life. (Mark 8:34–35 NLT)

Today we don't have to deny having been with Jesus. And it's not that we have a freedom to be Christians that didn't exist in the Roman empire. It is that no one would ever accuse us of being Christians. No one would even suspect it. When our lives show nothing of Jesus in our daily walk, there is not enough evidence to convict us of having been with Him. When we try to live our Christian lives in our own strength and power, we propagate a miserable failure. We play-act Christianity on Sunday mornings and during midweek services or Bible studies, but the rest of the time we are focused on getting our fleshly desires satisfied in our own selfish way.

The world looks at this and judges our bitter fruit more honestly than those that call themselves the brothers and sisters to whom we should be most answerable for our actions. We don't hold each other accountable because we don't want to be held accountable ourselves. Our "fellowship" and "communities of faith" are often just social clubs for those desiring to climb the religious ladder of "the respect of other people." We have very little to do with what God really wants done on the earth today. Our hypocrisy is the greatest thing Satan has going to build his kingdom—encounter by encounter, relationship by relationship, soul by soul.

Yet when one person dares to spend time with Jesus and starts to live out His present-day ministry, it can change an entire generation.

Around the turn of the twentieth century, students at a Bible school in Topeka, Kansas, started to spend time with Jesus and His Word, and a revival broke out on the campus. After searching the Scriptures for what it meant to be "filled with the Holy Spirit," they could find nothing to indicate that it was not for their day nor any valid evidence that the gifts of the Spirit were not for all believers. At this revelation, one of the students stepped forward and asked that hands be laid on her—as was done for believers in Acts 8:14–17—that she might receive the infilling of the Holy Spirit. When this was done, she was instantly filled and began speaking in tongues just as they did in Samaria roughly nineteen centuries earlier. Soon everyone in the school was filled.

Eventually this blessing touched the life of William Seymour, a poor, one-eyed, demoralized African-American living before the civil rights movement was even a dream. This touch on his life inspired him to spend time with Jesus. This unknown man started holding meetings in a burned-out mission building on Azusa Street. From this came a revival that has proven to be one of the greatest strategic victories in Christian history. The Gospel was *experienced,* not just heard, through the gifts of the Spirit, when it was embraced in the hearts of the believers. The Pentecostal movement that began with those meetings has touched many elements of the body of Christ and at the end of the century was still the fastest-growing part of Jesus' body on the earth today.

Just as this movement at the beginning of the twentieth century continued to touch His church until the close of that century, God is today looking for men and women who will get real with Him and spend time with Him so that He can touch His church afresh *through them* in the twenty-first century. He is looking for those willing to be part of the answer to Jesus' prayers.

This can never happen until we fully plug ourselves in to the source of all answered prayer. Time spent at church services, Bible studies, listening to teaching tapes or CDs, watching Christian programming, reading Christian books, or whatever other things we might do to learn about God are good things, but they cannot replace our time spent with Jesus. We spend too much time flying by the seat of our pants spiritually and not enough time on our knees physically. I would even venture to say that if you don't spend time praying every day, then you don't believe in God as much as whatever it is that you spend your time doing. You can make an idol out of anything you place in a position of worship through your constant attention to it if it is greater than the attention you give God! It is time we got back to our first loves and let the lukewarmness be washed from our lives by being in and filled with the presence of God!

In the early years of my ministry, I made the circuit of Full Gospel Businessmen's meetings, giving them the only part of my testimony I could bear to admit at the time and trying to become a "superstar" as the Jewish boy who was converted. Standing in my pinstriped suit in a hotel ballroom one day, I was praying with people when Jesus quietly said, "Get out of here." I argued, as usual, because I didn't believe it was proper for the guest minister to run out on the prayer line, but I finally submitted and left.

Out on the busy New York street, I felt impressed to walk several blocks and then kneel. It was so embarrassing; I knelt on one knee as if to tie my shoelaces, even though I was wearing loafers without laces. But the person of the Holy Spirit weighed heavily on me. I finally knelt on both knees and began to cry almost uncontrollably. God was breaking that pinstriped showoff who thought he was so important he couldn't leave the prayer line. Jesus softly said, "Son, your obedience in your private life letermine the degree of My anointing on your public life."

The crowds had continued to shuffle past me throughout this episode, but as I arose, one scruffy-looking man carrying two bottles of wine pointed at me and said, "You're weird." It must be God when the weird people call you weird!

Like the little child Jesus called to himself and who came so simply, without question or regard to what he had been doing, we must obey His prompting in our private lives before His strength will manifest itself in our public lives. This can only come from spending time with Him.

Have you been with Jesus?

Living *His* Life

God wants us to live and breathe in Him. The Lord of Glory knows why we don't. We read and pray. We attend church. Whether we know it or not, we practice empty rituals just as the Pharisees and Sadducees did in Jesus' day. We've been bound by the lie that we have to struggle to live the Christian life rather than letting Christ live it through us—that God is not going to use us in a big way as He did the early disciples because that was only for their time, or we are not as holy as they were, or any of the million other excuses we use to keep us from the perfect will of God.

Wrong! Jesus will show up big time in hungry saints to gather the final harvest. They will form the army described in the book of Joel that will live the end-time ministry of Jesus on the earth. Will you be part of that army?

Why allow the person of the Holy Spirit to pass over us? He can only use those willing to take the next step and die to their flesh. If we are willing to take this step, then we can be part of the end-time ministry of Jesus!

Status-quo holy-Joe Christianity doesn't work; only Christ-centered Christianity does. We need a vibrant relationship with a living God that will allow His power to change our lives and the lives of those around us. This is a Christianity worth living for—and worth dying for.

God wants us to work holy, living works just as Jesus did. Works that reach souls. Why else would Jesus have told us that believers would do His works?

Shouldn't there be some way—other than Christian T-shirts—that people know we have been with Jesus? Shouldn't being with Jesus somehow make us different? Make us stand out?

God is looking to do great things through us if we are only willing to be with Him and walk where He tells us to walk. Spending time with Jesus is not something we do and are done with until another time; it is something we live breath by breath.

Carving Out Quiet

How does such a vibrant relationship come? Just how does one "spend time with Jesus?" Is it just a matter of spending hours praying in the Spirit? Is it a matter of meditating on every verse in the Word of God that we come across? Is it praising Him at the top of our voices? Or weeping before Him in repentance?

All of these may happen in a time of coming before the Lord, but they are not in themselves spending time with Jesus. We can do these things just as easily in our flesh as any other religious practice we put ourselves through to make us feel better about ourselves. Truly spending time with Jesus is coming to a place of spiritual attentiveness and being quiet before Him so that we can hear His voice clearly, learn the details of obedience, and let His Spirit cut away the chaff in our lives so that we can bear the fruit He has planned for us to bear. It is a quietness of spirit that comes from being able to focus on God. This often comes after times of prayer, repentance, meditation on the Scriptures, and/or praise. It is a place where we have quieted the self and all the voices of this world to focus solely on seeking His face. God said through the psalmist:

> Be still, and know that I am God: I will be exalted among the heathen, I will be exalted in the earth. (Psalm 46:10)

The Hebrew word translated "still" here is *raphah,* which means "to relax, sink down, let drop, be disheartened . . . withdraw . . . abandon, refrain, forsake . . . to be quiet."[6] Four of the major translations of this word elsewhere in the King James Version are "feeble," "frail," "weaken," and "alone." It seems to have a note of surrender, silence, and abandonment in it.

Being with Jesus is a matter of letting all other things drop, setting all else aside, and focusing only on Him. There is a singularity, a simplicity, and a vulnerability that go with it. It is not something that can be done in five minutes. It may take more than hours at first. It may demand a quiet weekend retreat away every once in a while. But it is also a place that is easier to get to with practice, though it also gets deeper and deeper the more you go there. It is being before God alone in perfect honesty and seeking Him and His kingdom with all of our hearts. It is a place of resting and trusting in Him more than anything else, knowing that His ways are above our own, and of sitting in His presence as children sitting with their Father. It is a place of comfort and correction, instruction and intercession, sincere seeking and profound finding. It is the place where we are open to letting God touch our lives and touch the lives of others through ours. It is a state of being constantly open and attentive to God while being vigilant to avoid distractions.

Busyness Is a Temptation!

In our modern society of promote-and-acquire push and shove, a place of such quietness seems unnatural. Even for those of us who do carve out some quiet time, that time is often spent going over busy schedules, trying to make sense of all we are doing, rather than truly focusing on God. Then in the midst of all of this, we lapse somehow from even that little time alone with God because of the urgency of so much of what we do. There are so many problems around us that we think only we can solve, whether it is at work, at home, or even in the church we attend. The telephone rings, someone turns on the TV in the next room, the radio is blaring, etc. We are too exhausted most of the time to even focus. When we finally do get some quiet time to ourselves, the last thing we want to do is open our Bibles and study or seek the Lord in prayer for an hour. We want to be distracted and entertained. We think it is only right for us to be able to check out for a little while during our downtime. We don't think about what we are doing as we collapse on the couch in front of the TV "just to see what's on." Then we flick through the channels for an hour or two, watching nothing but the changing images as we go. After that, when we are too tired to do anything else, we trudge off to bed.

Time before and after church gets lost in catching up on the latest gossip. Problems at home or work are the talk of the day. The drum of busyness beats faster and faster, and we dance through a choreographed chaos that allows us anything but a quiet moment of reflection or thought. We react more than we act. Decisions are made by habit rather than consideration. We choose to follow what other people say rather than finding out the truth for ourselves because the former is so much easier. Our doctrine becomes whatever the preacher says, and we even stop opening our Bibles to follow along with the Scriptures as he is teaching, just taking for granted that he or she is quoting everything in context.

Then we work ourselves until we drop to fulfill the goals and purposes of others—whether at work or at church—often only to find that their true aims were not the ideals we signed on to promote. This disappointment and discouragement often lapses into bitterness, then self thrives as the ego becomes more dominant, and Jesus gets pushed further and further to the fringes of our lives by this and other fleshly fruit. Religion (a dead list of rules and regulations) becomes easier than reality (a vibrant relationship with Jesus) to live by. A little fleshly indulgence seems more and more justifiable because it feels like such a needed relief from all our hard work. After all, look at how much we have accomplished!

Yet the truth is that we have replaced accomplishment with

activity and mistaken busyness and urgency for importance. We race faster and faster to do things of less and less significance to the kingdom of God. And because of this, all we have to look forward to will be digging up our single talent one day, still caked with dirt, and holding it before Jesus, smiling as we say, "See, Lord, I still have it! Here it is!" He will only look at us, weeping and shaking His head, to say, "Oh, you wicked and slothful servant . . ."

Satan couldn't be happier with all we do!

The Bible, however, tells us that we can be too busy and too wrapped up in things other than what God has for us:

> *Study to be quiet,* and to do your own business, and to work with your own hands, as we commanded you; That ye may walk honestly toward them that are without, and that ye may have lack of nothing. (1 Thessalonians 4:11–12)

Here the word "quiet" is the Greek word *hesuchazo,* which means "to rest, cease from labor . . . to lead a quiet life, said of those who are not running hither and thither, but stay at home and mind their business."[7] Those who spend time with Jesus regularly have a simplicity and focus to their lives that helps them avoid pitfalls and getting caught up in the wrong things. They find a place of rest in Christ.

The fact is we are much busier as a rule than we need to be. We could be half as busy and accomplish twice as much if we would slow down and really spend time with Jesus! God has no heavy burdens for us!

> Come unto me, all ye that labor and are heavy laden, and I will give you rest. Take my yoke upon you, and learn of me; for I am meek and lowly in heart: and ye shall find rest unto your souls. For my yoke is easy, and my burden is light. (Matthew 11:28–30)

We are wasting our time trying to live our lives in the flesh with its limited strength!

Those plugged into Jesus are not overworked and stressed out all the time. The work of God is not too much to bear. God has help and rest for His people. We just never seem to enter into it because we put more faith in ourselves than we do in Jesus.

God's promise of entering his place of rest still stands, so we ought to tremble with fear that some of you might fail to get there. For this Good News—that God has prepared a place of rest—has been announced to us just as it was to them [the people of Israel in the desert with Moses]. But *it did them no good because they didn't believe what God told them.* . . .

For all who enter into God's rest will find rest from *their labors,* just as God rested after creating the world. Let us do our best to enter that place of rest. For anyone who disobeys God, as the people of Israel did, will fall.

For the word of God is full of living power. It is sharper than the sharpest knife, cutting deep into our innermost thoughts and desires. *It exposes us for what we really are.* Nothing in all creation can hide from him. Everything is naked and exposed before his eyes. This is the God to whom we must explain all that we have done.

That is why we have a great High Priest who has gone to heaven, Jesus the Son of God. Let us cling to him and never stop trusting him. This High Priest of ours understands our weaknesses, for he faced all of the same temptations we do, yet he did not sin. *So let us come boldly to the throne of our gracious God. There we will receive his mercy, and we will find grace to help us when we need it.* (Hebrews 4:1–2, 10–16 NLT)

Those who enter into His rest cease from their labors and pick up those of Jesus, whose burden is light. They have time for work, but they also have time for other things: family, church, and, yes, even leisure activities. It is never God's desire to burn you out. In fact, it has been my experience that God loves the minister more than the ministry and that if He has to shut down a church to save the faithful pastor from working him- or herself to death, He will. I have even seen ministers resist Him in this, thinking they were being godly! If this is the way God feels about it, how much more should we prize and protect the gifts He has given us in the people who work in our ministries?[8] If we were truly being godly, there would never be people abused and overworked in our churches.

> *Those who enter into His rest cease from their labors and pick up those of Jesus, whose burden is light.*

This rest is also a result of the Word of God working in us to cut away those things that are worthless or evil for the sake of those things that bear eternal fruit pleasing to Him. This is the place of intense honesty before God where we will let His Word expose which things are fleshly and which are godly—it will show us how we really are! It will tear away self's shroud of deception and help us to see things clearly. It will expose ills in the light of truth, allowing us to cut away wasteful, decaying fruit and nurture life-giving fruit. We will no longer delude ourselves into thinking that we are more than we really are, and our judgment will be more sound as we strive for the perfect will of God.

> Therefore I urge you, brethren, by the mercies of God, to present your bodies a living and holy sacrifice, acceptable to God, which is your spiritual service of worship. And *do not be conformed to this world,* but be transformed by the renewing of your mind, *so that you may prove what the will of God is,* that which is good and acceptable and perfect. For through the grace given to me *I say to everyone among you not to think more highly of himself than he ought to think; but to think so as to have sound judgment, as God has allotted to each a measure of faith.* (Romans 12:1–3 NASB)

We are commanded not to conform to this world and the way it functions—we are to be in the world but not of the world.[9]

This means that while we exist in a world that is frantic and over-stressed, we do not need to bear these pressures on our own. We can instead be focused on doing our part of what God has called us to do and enjoy God's help in doing it. It is interesting to note that the above passage comes just before a section talking about how the body of Christ is to work together in its parts:

> For just as we have many members in one body and all the members do not have the same function, so we, who are many, are one body in Christ, and individually members one of another. Since we have gifts that differ according to the grace given to us, each of us is to exercise them accordingly. (Romans 12:4–6 NASB)

God doesn't expect us to do it all alone, but He does expect us to do it all together, each carrying out our own part and lifting the burdens of one another. There will be a time for rest, while there will also be times for busyness, but with all this comes the grace to overcome. Never worry that you aren't doing enough, but do be concerned that you are not doing what you are supposed to do. *This is where the peace and rest of God resides: in the continual presence of Jesus as we do His perfect will.*

Pray Without Ceasing

Though being with Jesus does start with times of getting alone with Him and His Word regularly, if you leave Jesus in your prayer closet or quiet place, you are still missing out on His ministry. Just as there is a place for getting quiet with God, there is a place of taking Him out of the quiet place and into the world—after all, how else will we help others if we don't take Him to them?

Paul admonishes us in the book of Thessalonians to "pray without ceasing."[10] Does he mean to be continually on our knees in our prayer closet and never come out? No. I believe it means taking the attitude and attentiveness of prayer with us wherever we go. Nothing should come out of our mouths that we wouldn't

THE UNANSWERED PRAYERS OF JESUS

say to God in prayer. No situation we meet should pass by unsolved without its being set before the throne of God. We should also be ever ready for God to speak to our hearts about what to do and how to solve such problems.

When you take time to be with Jesus, He will take time to go where you go and bring His power and wisdom with Him.

So I ask again, "Have you been with Jesus *today?*"

Well, now is always the best time to start!

Behold, I stand at the door, and knock: if any man hear my voice, and open the door, I will come in to him, and will sup with him, and he with me. To him that over-cometh will I grant to sit with me in my throne, even as I also overcame, and am set down with my Father in his throne. He that hath an ear, let him hear what the Spirit saith unto the churches. (Revelation 3:20–22)

CHAPTER TEN

The *Greater* Commandment

That the love wherewith thou hast loved me may be in them.

JOHN 17:26

This is my commandment, that ye love one another, as I have loved you.

JOHN 15:12

A woman came to Jesus with a costly box of perfume called spikenard, worth an entire year's wages. She broke the box directly on Christ's head so as to use up every drop of the precious oil. The religious men who witnessed this grumbled that she'd wasted money, but Jesus was so moved, He said that wherever His gospel was preached, the story of her offering would be told.[1]

The box she broke wasn't itself the fragrant offering for Jesus. The woman didn't paint or polish the box to try to make it more acceptable to Him before she broke it to release its contents. She didn't try to get the box to smell like the perfume inside. Instead, she smashed the box so the purity of the nard inside could be released.

It is time we stopped paying so much attention to our outer selves and start focusing on the most precious Christ within us. It is only through releasing Jesus within us that the world will experience His kingdom.

We Cannot Love Like Jesus Until We Are Broken Like Jesus

Jesus' ninth and final unanswered prayer in John 17 was "that your love for me may be in them."[2] I believe that He didn't just pray this so that this love could stay bottled up inside us, because He also commanded us to "love one another, as I have loved you."[3] Love bottled up inside of us is of little use to anyone, no matter how much we dress up the outside of the bottle. Though we as Christians have this love within us from the time we are born again—"because the love of God is shed abroad in our hearts by the Holy Ghost which is given unto us"[4]—most of us are so *self*-involved and *self*-absorbed that we never experience God's incredible love for us.

> *Where selfishness is the rule, there is no place for the love of God to work.*

Where selfishness is the rule, there is no place for the love of God to work. Self on the throne is diametrically opposed to the love of God that Paul describes in 1 Corinthians 13. Look at each of the points Paul brings out about the love of God in this passage:

Love is patient,
love is kind and is not jealous;
love does not brag and is not arrogant,
does not act unbecomingly;
it does not seek its own,
is not provoked,
does not take into account a wrong suffered,
does not rejoice in unrighteousness,
but rejoices with the truth;
bears all things,
believes all things,
hopes all things,
endures all things.
Love never fails.
(1 Corinthians 13:4–8 NASB)

Paul describes the love of God as the most powerful force in the universe—something that never fails. No wonder Christians today are so powerless to change our society—we have forgotten to exercise our unfailing power source.

In Ephesians 5, Paul uses the marriage relationship as an analogy for the relationship between Christ and His church.[5] Somehow—in a time when more than 50 percent of marriages end in divorce—this remains a perfect description of the state of the church today. The major reason we divorce each other is the same reason most of us are "divorced" from Christ. As selfishness and love for "the outside of the box" kills marriages, it also kills the mission of today's church.

Love is the oil that lubricates the parts and joints Ephesians 4:16 describes. Without it the friction between us chafes and grates. If this goes on for long the pieces are misshapen, burned out, and separated; the effectiveness of the body of Christ grinds to a halt. Instead of operating like a well-oiled machine, ushering in the kingdom of God, all we do is produce smoke that blinds the eyes of those we are trying to teach the truth. Just as love never fails, *without* love we always fail.

Releasing the Life of God

For the life of God to be released through Jesus Christ, God himself had to come to the earth *and die*. We are followers of Christ's pattern. Our outer shell—the natural man—has to die in order for the inner man to be released. As long as we try to preserve the outer shell—keeping the flesh-life intact—the inner man will never be released. As long as we are enamored by our outer shell, we will never see the ministry of Jesus Christ live through us.

The Christian life is to be lived in the Spirit, not the flesh. We must

> *As long as we are enamored by our outer shell, we will never see the ministry of Jesus Christ live through us.*

crucify the flesh, mortify the members of our flesh, and die to self so the Spirit of God can rule and reign in our lives. The Bible says it's like a seed that falls into the ground and dies, only to spring up again.

> A grain of wheat must fall to the ground and die to make many seeds. But if it never dies, it remains only a single seed. Those who love their lives will lose them, but those who hate their lives in this world will keep true life forever. (John 12:24–25 NCV)

A seed is a container of life. As long as this container remains alone, it cannot grow. Some seeds sit for decades with no growth and seemingly no purpose, until something breaks open the outer shell so the seed can interact with the soil and water. Once this happens, it begins to grow. A seed can sit for a hundred years in its own identity and accomplish nothing. But when a seed finally dies, the life that comes from that one seed can feed millions.

We spend all of our time and efforts trying to be loved and miss the fact that we already have the most powerful love in the universe ready to burst out of us. We keep looking to the clouds hoping for Jesus to come back in the flesh as He sits in our prayer closets waiting for us to come in and spend time with Him. The eternal fate of all those around us rests on our ability to look past the temporal and temporary and live our Christianity as if we really believed in the heavenly and eternal!

Christian Fiction

It is amazing how much the popularity of Christian fiction has grown in recent years. From being a genre with little attention it has grown to engulf the *New York Times* bestseller list. It would be easy to condemn this as being a distraction from reading the Bible or even Christian discipleship books that are designed to lead us closer to God, but if we look more closely at the trend, I think we will see that it reveals a deeper hunger for God in the church today than we ever realized existed.

Why do I say this? How could it be that made-up stories show us anything about ourselves? Well, look at what these books are about. The *Left Behind* series has put out one top-selling book after another, and fictional stories of spiritual warfare continue to sell year after year. Others write books along the same themes that have probably made the fiction section in the local Christian bookstore the fastest expanding section of all. Why is this?

I believe it is because Christians today are incredibly hungry to see the supernatural power of God working in our everyday lives, and these books offer an opportunity to at least imagine living such a life. While the characters of these books walk through the end times or periods of spiritual significance that we feel so far removed from, we can vicariously imagine ourselves living with God active in our own lives.

> *There are more people on the earth today that need to make the decision between heaven and hell than in all history previous to the twentieth century combined!*

The only problem is that we *are* living in the end times and *now* is the greatest period of spiritual significance that the world has yet seen. There are more people on the earth today that need to make the decision between heaven and hell than in all history previous to the twentieth century combined! *It is time for us to stop living vicariously through fiction and start living God's will for real.*

Fully Armed, Equipped, and Ready to Bail Out

So many Christians I have come across in my travels are like F-16 Eagle pilots who zoom around in the world's most powerfully equipped airplanes, every Sunday showing off incredible feats of "operating in the heavenlies." Yet at the first speck of trouble on the radar come Monday, they are groping for the eject button. "Oh, brother," they say, "won't it be wonderful when Jesus finally comes back and raptures us out of this place and we can be with

Him? Don't we truly have something to look forward to?"

Yes, we do have something wonderful to look forward to, but why only look forward to it when we can be living it today? Why wait for Jesus to come back when He is already here? Why look for another time of miracles on the earth when He wants so badly to perform them now? The only eject button we need to be looking for is the button that will eject our self out of the pilot seat so that we can turn that seat back over to Jesus!

When we hear the word *egotistical,* we often think of some-one who pushes others around trying to get his way. While this is one part of being egotistical, to me it is a small part. Being ego-tistical actually means we reject what God says about us because we believe more in our own opinion of things. We look into the Bible and say, "Well, yeah, that's true, but He must really mean that for someone else, not me." We say, "I can't," "I shouldn't," "I'm not worthy to," "I would never dare," etc. We think we are being humble, but instead we are operating in the worst kind of pride—the kind that says we know more than God does!

If we spend time with Him in His Word, we can begin to see more clearly what God has for us. James calls the Word of God a mirror that will show us who we really are in Christ. If we refuse to do what we learn in such times of being with Jesus, then we are like someone who looks into that mirror and walks away from it, immediately forgetting what he looks like.[6] This is looking fully into the face of God and saying, "No, God, that's not the way it is; it's really like this."

We can't afford to let our weaknesses and ignorance hinder His strength.

I was once headed to preach at a crusade in Cuba when, in the darkness, I missed seeing a six-foot-high concrete arch. Being five inches taller than that, I hit it full force and split my head, causing me to bleed profusely and see double through the entire message. (What a massive crowd!)

The next morning we flew to Amsterdam to witness in the red-light district, and my head was pounding with the worst migraine imaginable. We landed, went out to Baines Bridge, and I asked the team to join me in prayer because I was in too much blinding pain and too exhausted to minister. As we gathered in a circle, holding hands and praying, prostitutes, drug addicts, and homosexuals started walking up to see who was in the center of the circle. More and more came until, when we turned around, a large crowd of people surrounded us. I don't know how many were saved that night, but it was a miracle. I discovered later I had suffered a severe concussion. By then it didn't matter.

Now, am I saying that even if you are badly injured you still need to go out and minister for God no matter what? No, don't misunderstand why I am sharing this story. If you hurt yourself you still need to have wisdom and get help, which is exactly what I did once I realized I'd received a concussion! What I am saying is that we often neglect to serve God because we feel we are too weak or not smart enough, not realizing that admitting this is more of a help than a hindrance. Our weaknesses make room for His strengths. God is looking to do great things through us, if we are only willing to be with Him and walk where He tells us to walk—and let His love flow through us.

What Can Separate Us From the Love of God?

Ego on the throne has hindered the operation of this love in our lives. Whether we insist on our own way or hide "humbly" behind our inabilities—and thus reject God's abilities—we are letting our ego remain firmly on the throne of our lives and deceive ourselves in thinking we are doing right. Susanna Wesley, the mother of revivalists John and Charles Wesley, once said, "Religion is nothing else than doing the will of God and not our own. Heaven or hell depends on this alone." It is just that simple. Yet instead of doing God's will every day, we smother truth and love by wrapping it tightly in jargon and justifications for our inactivity and disobedience: "Oh, it is so hard to live a Christian life!" It is not *hard* to live a Christian life—it is *impossible*! That is why we have to let Jesus live it through us.

Ego dressed in this cloak of religion is poison. It is the pro-verbial wolf in sheep's clothing. We must empty ourselves of this ego—the big "I"—every day. We must come to the mirror, look into it long and hard, and then not forget what we saw when we walk away. The deposit of the Father's love within us is hindered by our ego. Only by smashing this false exterior can we release His love to those around us. That love is what keeps the present-day ministry of Christ flowing through us and oils the points where we come into contact with others in His body so that we can all effectively work together to manifest His kingdom on earth.

Too often, however, the opposite is true. Shrouded in our cloak of religious egotism, we practice "sanctified revenge." We stab those that oppose or rival us in the back "in the name of Jesus" because they have threatened or intimidated us. We find a way to turn away from them, claiming that we are justified. It is at that point the joints and parts have been smoking for some time from the friction, and they are starting to come apart.

Things from without cannot keep us from the love of God, only things from within. Look at what Paul said about this at the end of Romans 8:

> We know that God causes everything to work together for the good of those who love God and are called accord-ing to his purpose for them. For God knew his people in advance, and he chose them to become like his Son, so that his Son would be the firstborn, with many brothers and sisters. And having chosen them, he called them to come to him. And he gave them right standing with himself, and he promised them his glory.
>
> What can we say about such wonderful things as these? If God is for us, who can ever be against us? Since God did not spare even his own Son but gave him up for us all, won't God, who gave us Christ, also give us everything else? . . .
>
> Can anything ever separate us from Christ's love? Does it mean he no longer loves us if we have trouble or calam-

ity, or are persecuted, or are hungry or cold or in danger or threatened with death? (Even the Scriptures say, "For your sake we are killed every day; we are being slaughtered like sheep.") No, despite all these things, overwhelming victory is ours through Christ, who loved us.

And I am convinced that nothing can ever separate us from his love. Death can't, and life can't. The angels can't, and the demons can't. Our fears for today, our worries about tomorrow, and even the powers of hell can't keep God's love away. Whether we are high above the sky or in the deepest ocean, nothing in all creation will ever be able to separate us from the love of God that is revealed in Christ Jesus our Lord. (Romans 8:28–32, 35–39 NLT)

No, nothing can separate us from His love, but we can refuse to release it in our lives by letting it be smothered in our own fleshly pursuits. We halt the work of God and reject Jesus' prayer by ignoring the *greater* commandment, that we love one another as He has loved us.

Without releasing this love, we will never do the greater works—or even the same works—that Jesus did. It is time we activated this last prayer of Jesus and released the love He has so bountifully poured on us to the world around us. This love is the foundation of His kingdom. It is time that we started to live its reality and release it to those around us. Then watch what happens. Jesus' works are much closer than you have ever imagined!

CHAPTER ELEVEN

Will You Be Part of the Answers to Jesus' Prayers?

Verily, verily, I say unto you, He that believeth on me, the works that I do shall he do also; and greater works than these shall he do; because I go to my Father.

JOHN 14:12

If two of you shall agree on earth as touching any thing that they shall ask, it shall be done for them of my Father which is in heaven. For where two or three are gathered together in my name, there am I in the midst of them.

MATTHEW 18:19–20

There is a unique calling from God on your life. He has a plan for your life that He has for no one else. What you do with it is up to you. Will you bury it in the ground like the servant with one talent?[1] Or will you come into agreement with Jesus' prayers and be part of their answer? Will you continue to live with self on the throne—with its hurts, its ego, its deficiencies, its selfishness, its deception, and its clouded, narrow-minded worldview ruling your life? Though the issues of knowing and living God's plan for your life may seem complex, the actual decision is really very basic: Will you live this day—this hour, this minute, this breath—with Jesus as the Lord of your life, or do you think you can do it better on your own?

This is the moment to make that decision—this moment and every moment following for the rest of your life. It may sound hard, but I wouldn't want to live any other way!

Recently I heard about a football player who had the personal motto: "No one will work harder than I do today." It was a motto that took him to Harvard on an academic scholarship when he was born into a family that never could have afforded it otherwise. This motto brought him to a starting position on an NFL team even though Harvard is rarely a place NFL scouts find great talent.

We should have a similar motto that is just as simple: "Today I will seek God in order to do His will."

One of Satan's greatest tricks is to make living a Christlike life look beyond reach. He would have us idolize certain men and women of God like a teenager may idolize a rock star or a sports hero. He would have us think, *Oh, if I could only be like them! But it must take such great talent and determination to do what they do. It is so far beyond anything I could ever do!*

> *One of Satan's greatest tricks is to make living a Christlike life look beyond reach.*

Well, there is the deception. *If I could only be like them.* Well, guess what? You are like them! If you are a Christian, then you have the same Holy Spirit on the inside of you that they have on the inside of them; you have the same Jesus as Lord and Savior, and you have the same Father who loves you and wants to know and be known by you. *In His eyes, all that matters is your obedience to His will.* Large meetings don't matter. Big churches don't matter. Incredible mission outreaches don't matter. If they are of God, then they are merely byproducts of believers who have obeyed Him. The important thing is the obedience.

> Except the LORD build the house, they labor in vain
> that build it: except the LORD keep the city, the watchman

waketh but in vain. It is vain for you to rise up early, to sit up late, to eat the bread of sorrows: for so he giveth his beloved sleep. (Psalm 127:1–2)

We can work hard, stay up late, rise early, and work at the church 120 out of 168 hours in the week, but none of this matters if we are building a kingdom to ourselves rather than to God. In fact, the opposite is true: If we are obeying God, then we won't be working impossibly long hours to build His kingdom, because He gives His beloved sleep and rest. The only real work is staying in our quiet place until we learn His will and how to do it. Then we simply have to walk it out. The rest will take care of itself.

We need to come into agreement with God and His Word. We need to come into agreement with Jesus' prayers.

The Power of Agreement

The works of Jesus—and the greater works—will only come to the church when we as Christians come into agreement with His Word, His will, and His nine unanswered prayers from John 17. We need to seek His face sincerely to know what He wants us to do. God is waiting for those who dare to draw close to Him. Are you willing to get authentic with God and press in to Him until Jesus' nine prayers are really and truly answered?

(1) "That they may know the only true God."[2]

We cannot be content with knowing *about God* or *what others think of God*. This is dead religion and self-worship. We have to take the risk of spending time with Jesus and His Word ourselves and get to really know Him, His heart, His ministry for the earth today, and then just do it. We will never know God until we seek Him with all of our hearts.

> "You will seek Me and find Me when you search for Me with all your heart. I will be found by you," declares the LORD. (Jeremiah 29:13–14 NASB)

(2) "That they may be one."[3]

Division has come from not being one with Jesus. If we were all one with Jesus we would all take our proper place in His body. If we are ever to have unity in the church, it will not be through ecumenical movements that water down the truth in order to be more accepting of others. Only when we are one with Jesus will we be one with each other. Each of us must first learn our individual place in His plan. Only then can each part be "fitly joined together"[4] to realize His kingdom on earth.

> Under his direction, the whole body is fitted together perfectly. As each part does its own special work, it helps the other parts grow, so that the whole body is healthy and growing and full of love. (Ephesians 4:16 NLT)

(3) "That they might have my joy."[5]

We don't have His joy because we are trying to live by our flesh and its deceptive desires. His joy is not a fruit of the flesh but a fruit of His Spirit[6] and it comes from doing His will. When we live by His Spirit and give Him our emotions and desires, there is nothing the devil can do to us to steal our peace and joy. We have "joy unspeakable and full of glory"[7] because we celebrate with the Christ within us as we are part of manifesting His kingdom on the earth.

> When you obey me, you remain in my love, just as I obey my Father and remain in his love. I have told you this so that you will be filled with my joy. Yes, your joy will overflow! (John 15:10–11 NLT)

(4) "That you shouldest keep them from evil."[8]

Proverbs says, "The complacency of fools will destroy them."[9] When we become comfortable in our flesh or accept its dictates that, for one reason or another, we cannot live like Jesus, then we give evil free reign in both our own lives and our communities. We take the tone, "Well, there is really nothing I can do about it—I wonder what's on TV tonight." We accept being entertained rather than fulfilled. This is complacency. This is spiritual poverty.

If we are ever to be a threat to evil rather than having evil be a threat to us, then we must learn that our new nature in Christ has also given us a *new* past, a *new* culture, and a *new* life—and that because of these things we have a *new* supernatural present and future! Simple childlike obedience to His direction can usher in His present-day ministry and vanquish evil as He establishes His will and His kingdom on the earth around us.

> My brothers, be all the more eager to make your calling and election sure. *For if you do these things, you will never fall,* and you will receive a rich welcome into the eternal kingdom of our Lord and Savior Jesus Christ. (2 Peter 1:10–11 NIV)

(5) "That they might be sanctified through the truth."[10]

Do we live by truth? Are we brutally honest with ourselves at all times? Are we willing to go through Christ's daily pruning to cut off that which is dead so that we may bear more fruit?[11] Loving the truth is key to living out Jesus' present-day ministry on the earth. Those who believe or swallow half-truths lapse into complacency and self-contentment. They are satisfied with where they are and don't care about pressing in to seek God's will and His desires.

People who love truth are not afraid of letting others see their weaknesses or humanity. In fact, they are able to glorify God, as His strength can be seen through their weakness! It is not a "special anointing" that counts but having been with the Anointed One—Jesus Christ.[12]

> Since God has so generously let us in on what he is doing, we're not about to throw up our hands and walk off the job just because we run into occasional hard times. We refuse to wear masks and play games. We don't maneuver and manipulate behind the scenes. And we don't twist God's Word to suit ourselves. Rather, *we keep everything we do and say out in the open, the whole truth on display, so*

that those who want to can see and judge for themselves in the presence of God. (2 Corinthians 4:1–2 THE MESSAGE)

(6) "That they may behold my glory."[13]

God's glory has appeared on the earth as men, women, and children have humbled themselves before God, sincerely sought His presence, and repented of their fleshly lives. But repentance alone has never been able to keep God's glory and revival growing. It has always been limited to a certain place for a certain time. It has always been quenched when we have turned back to our flesh for the answers, thinking we can discipline it into eternity.

> *It is time for a generation that will forsake the flesh and rise to walk in the Spirit empowered by His gifts and gifted by His power.*

The Bible is clear on this: It is not what we *don't* do, it is what we *do*. It is time for a generation that will forsake the flesh and rise to walk in the Spirit empowered by His gifts and gifted by His power. Only then will the fruit of His glory have a place to take root and flourish throughout the entire earth.

All of us have had that veil removed so that we can be mirrors that brightly reflect the glory of the Lord. And as the Spirit of the Lord works within us, we become more and more like him and reflect his glory even more. (2 Corinthians 3:18 NLT)

(7) "That they may be made perfect."[14]

The only perfect person is a dead person. We have been crucified, buried, and resurrected with Christ. It is no longer we who live but Christ who lives through us.[15] We must let that Christ-life flow through us so that we can be revived like the valley of dry bones was before Ezekiel.[16] Are we willing to leave the corpse of our flesh behind and go on with His Spirit into God's holiness and perfection, being made into a vessel "for the master's use"?[17]

Be sober, be vigilant; because your adversary the devil, as a roaring lion, walketh about, seeking whom he may devour: Whom resist steadfast in the faith, knowing that the same afflictions are accomplished in your brethren that are in the world.

But the God of all grace, who hath called us unto his eternal glory by Christ Jesus, after that ye have suffered a while, *make you perfect,* [e]stablish, strengthen, settle you. (1 Peter 5:8–10)

(8) *That the world would know that we have "been with Jesus."*[18]

The world knew that the apostles had been with Jesus. Peter's shadow glowed from having been with Jesus.[19] And lest we think that walking the earth with Jesus was the only way to qualify for walking in the anointing of Jesus, remember, Paul spread even more of Christ around the world than did the Twelve, having only spent time with Jesus *after* His ascension.

It is time to press in to Him until the world sees Jesus shining in our faces and as a result is awakened from the sleep of self-deception, becoming born again.

When they saw the courage of Peter and John and realized that they were unschooled, ordinary men, they were astonished and they took note that these men had been with Jesus. (Acts 4:13 NIV)

(9) *"That the love with which you loved me may be in them."*[20]

As we reveal Christ to a desperate world, we reveal a supernatural love that embraces and heals the world. We can no longer be content to focus on the outside—polishing, painting, and admiring the outside of the box as if it were of more value than the perfume of His love that is within. It is time to shatter the worship of outward appearance and let what is inside of us flow forth: the love of God,[21] His righteousness, and His kingdom.[22] We cannot ignore Jesus' greater commandment—we must love others with the same love that Jesus loves us.

Beloved, let us love one another: for love is of God; and every one that loveth is born of God, and knoweth God. He that loveth not knoweth not God; for God is love. In this was manifested the love of God toward us, because that God sent his only begotten Son into the world, that we might live through him. (1 John 4:7–9)

Jesus Has Delegated It *to Us*!

As we join Christ in prayer, we gain the power to say, "Look on us," because we've been with Jesus. Alone with our Lord, we take on His characteristics. His presence and power makes demons tremble and mountains quake. The last great blow to the devil will be when the saints no longer appear as Joe, or Shirley, or Marco, or Latisha, but we all look just like Jesus—transformed because we've spent time with Him!

Who will do greater works than Jesus? People who are His representatives—who have seen Him, been with Him, and spent time with Him through prayer, meditating on His Word, praising Him, repenting from dead works, and being totally vulnerable before Him.

Jesus returned to the Father and is *sitting*. He is sitting because He has delegated His mission to you and me, and *He has faith that we will carry it out!*

Imagine God asking you to give everything you owned—including your name—to someone else who would do more with it than you would. Imagine giving your talent, your career, your family, your possessions, your reputation, everything you've ever been, plus everything you could potentially become, to another person, in the hope that they would accomplish more than you. That's exactly what God asked Jesus to do.

Jesus Christ delegated everything He had—His power, His reputation, His name, His life, His history, His words, His very Spirit, everything He'd ever been and everything He ever would be—and gave it to us.

Jesus Christ gave His ministry to the weakest believer in the body of Christ—the rights to His name, the keys to His kingdom, all His authority over the earth, and all power to represent Him on this earth. That weak person can abuse the power, misrepresent Christ's name, exploit His reputation, or choose not to do one thing with what Jesus gave—it is that person's choice. It is our choice as well.

> *Jesus Christ gave His ministry to the weakest believer in the body of Christ.*

Christ departed physically from the earth to sit—sit!—at the Father's right hand in heaven. Why? Jesus *knew*—beyond any shadow of doubt—there would come a day when the people who were called by His name would fulfill *all* His prophecies and bring about the answer to *all* His prayers: "Signs, wonders, and miracles will follow them that believe."[23]

The following verses are paraphrased:

"The works I've done shall you do and greater works than I shall you do because I go unto My Father."[24]

"If you ask anything in My name, My Father will do it."[25]

"If two agree as touching anything, it will be done."[26]

"Till we all come unto the measure of the stature of the fullness of Christ."[27]

"That they may be one, even as we are one: I in them, and thou in me, that they may be made perfect in one and that the world may know that thou hast sent Me."[28]

"That Christ may present the church to himself, as a glorious church, not having spot or wrinkle or any such thing; but that the church should be holy and without blemish."[29]

We haven't seen all His prayers answered or all His prophecies fulfilled, but we will. Christ's power resides within *us* as believers! We say at salvation, "Come into my heart, Lord Jesus." It's time to start believing He really did. When the ego of man is completely off the throne, and the barriers of our hearts come down, then the present-day ministry of Jesus Christ can be released. That's why Paul said, "I die daily,"[30] because he knew the self-life was the greatest enemy of the Cross.

Our Generation Will See Christ's Power

Jesus knew His death and resurrection was the greatest blow to Satan. The second greatest blow will come when believers, filled with Christ's Spirit, unite and multiply, allowing the present-day ministry of Jesus Christ to flow through and go beyond what we've ever seen or imagined.

Many years ago at the Waldorf Astoria in New York City, Prime Minister Begin, who won the Nobel Peace Prize, invited me to host the only Christian delegation with whom he would meet during that trip to the States. I invited thirty-two intercessors to join me. Ann Murchison, a wonderful Christian, Kyffin and Roberta Simpson, precious believers from Barbados, came, as did many others. While in the company of Prime Minister Begin, I asked Ann Murchison to read some Scriptures.

As she read, the presence of Jesus entered the room. Prime Minister Begin started weeping. We were still making introductions, and those who stood could hardly talk for weeping as well. The anointing grew so strong that the prime minister finally stood up and, with tears streaming down his face, said, "The Spirit I sense in this room is the Spirit of the redemption of Israel." All of those in the room had humbled themselves and become low before God. Christ was highly exalted and His glory filled the room. Everyone was weeping—Dr. Ben Armstrong, Executive Director of the National Religious Broadcasters; Forrest Montgomery, Attorney for the National Association of Evangelicals. The presence of God had filled the room. We could see the prophecy of King Solomon in 2 Chronicles 7:14: "If my people, who are called by my name, will humble themselves and pray and seek my face and turn from their wicked ways, then will I hear from heaven and will forgive their sin and will heal their land." It seemed as if the prophecy was being fulfilled before our very eyes. The Spirit the prime minister described was not only the Spirit of the redemption of Israel but of America also.

Yes, I can be with Jesus and I can be changed! You can be with Jesus and you can be changed! But we can't be changed until we admit what we're not and allow Jesus to be who He is through us, so in the divine fusion His life will be manifested.

We can preach repentance until we look like John the Baptist and still be a stench in the nostrils of God—intoxicated and drunk as a skunk on our own opinions. The living Christ in us has a divine schedule, a divine passion, and a divine purpose to manifest himself on this earth with the same blast of glory with which He manifested himself two thousand years ago.

The sole reason Jesus left this earth was to send His Spirit to us. "It is expedient for you that I go away: for if I go not away, the Comforter will not come unto you; but if I depart, I will send him unto you."[31] The ultimate mission of the person of the Holy Spirit is not to give us a gift. The great mission of the Holy Spirit is to manifest Jesus and all of His glory *in us* and *through us*!

When the Father sees Jesus abiding within us through His Spirit, all of heaven is authorized and mobilized to empower us to fulfill Christ's mission. Satan fears millions of us operating in the full measure of the Spirit of God, which will shatter his earthly reign.

When we've been with Jesus, we will be transformed into His likeness.[32] Satan cannot distinguish the face of Jesus from ours. Incredible authority and power comes upon us—the type of power Christ said would come, in which we would do greater works than He did.

Jesus testified He did only what He saw the Father do and spoke only what He heard the Father speak. *When we hear what Jesus hears and see what Jesus sees, we will do what Jesus did and speak with the authority that Jesus did.*

Jesus said, "I brought You glory on earth by completing the work You gave Me to do."[33] Christ's purpose was, and still is, to bring glory to the Father. Because Christ gave His ministry to us, our destiny is also to glorify God, which releases the power of heaven.

> And I will do whatever you ask in my name, so that the Son may bring glory to the Father. You may ask any-

thing in my name, and I will do it. (John 14:13–14 NIV)

Our generation will see the power Christ gave us manifested. Jesus fully intends to fulfill His present-day ministry. It's all about Jesus.

Jesus said, "Take up your cross and follow Me."[34]

Will you?

Bibliography

Achtemeier, Paul J. *Harper's Bible Dictionary*. 1st edition. San Francisco: Harper & Row, and Society of Biblical Literature, 1985.

Barrett, David B., George T. Kurian, and Todd M. Johnson, eds. *World Christian Encyclopedia: A Comparative Survey of Churches and Religions in the Modern World*. 2nd edition. New York: Oxford University Press, 2001.

Douglas, J. D. *New Bible Dictionary*. Wheaton, Ill.: Tyndale, 1996, 1982.

Merriam-Webster, Inc. *Merriam-Webster's Collegiate Dictionary*. 10th edition. Springfield, Mass.: Merriam-Webster, 1996, © 1993.

Strong, James. *Enhanced Strong's Lexicon*. Ontario: Woodside Bible Fellowship, 1996.

Vine, W. E., Merrill F. Unger, and William White. *Vine's Complete Expository Dictionary of Old and New Testament Words*. Volumes 1 & 2. Nashville: Thomas Nelson, 1996.

Endnotes

Introduction

1. Matthew 28:18–20 NCV.
2. See John 14:12.
3. See Mark 16:16–20.
4. John 17:20.
5. See Ephesians 4:13–16.

Chapter One

1. See Matthew 18:19.
2. John 16:7 NCV.
3. John 14:12 (emphasis mine).
4. As happened to Paul on the island of Malta in Acts 28:3–6.
5. See John 3:34.
6. See Mark 5:25–34.
7. See John 17:3.
8. See John 17:21.
9. See John 17:13.
10. See John 17:15.
11. See John 17:19.
12. See John 17:24.
13. See John 17:23.
14. See John 17:22–23, 25 and Acts 4:13.
15. See John 17:26.
16. Ephesians 5:27.
17. See 1 Timothy 2:3–4.
18. See Romans 10:9–10.
19. See Mark 16:20.

Chapter Two

1. See Genesis 15:7–17.
2. See Genesis 17:1–14.

3. See Genesis 18:22–33.
4. See Genesis 22:1–18.
5. W. E. Vine, Merrill F. Unger, and William White. *Vine's Complete Expository Dictionary of Old and New Testament Words,* Vol. 1. (Nashville: Thomas Nelson, 1996), s.v. "To know," 131.
6. See 1 Corinthians 3:1–3.
7. See Psalm 78:41.
8. Matthew 22:40.
9. John 14:12.
10. Ephesians 3:20.
11. See John 4:34.

Chapter Three

1. Hebrews 1:7.
2. John 17:11.
3. David B. Barrett, et al., eds., *World Christian Encyclopedia: A Comparative Survey of Churches and Religions in the Modern World,* Vol. 1., 2nd ed. (New York: Oxford University Press, 2001), 10.
4. If not, you can find the text online at *www.greatcom.org/laws/* or *www.crusade.org/fourlaws/.*
5. See 1 Corinthians 3:3.
6. See 1 Corinthians 1:6–7.
7. See Romans 8:1–9.
8. For example, the woman at the well in John 4, the Syrophenician woman in Mark 7:25–30, and the Roman centurion in Luke 7:1–10.
9. Vine, et al., Vol. 1., s.v. "Amen," 25.
10. See Matthew 13:31–32.
11. See Matthew 13:33.
12. See Matthew 13:44–46.
13. See Mark 10:23–26.
14. See Matthew 13:47–50.
15. See Matthew 20:1–16 and 22:2–14.
16. Vine, et al., Vol. 1, s.v. "Together," 263.

Chapter Four

1. See Nehemiah 7:73–8:18.
2. v. 13.
3. Matthew 10:8.

4. Vine, et al., Vol. 2, s.v. "Joy (Noun and Verb), Joyfulness, Joyfully, Joyous," 336.
5. See John 8:28, 38.
6. Hebrews 11:1.
7. See John 15:1–8.
8. See also Galatians 5:19–21.
9. See 2 Corinthians 10:12–14.
10. See Acts 16:22–26.
11. See Hebrews 13:5.
12. See Romans 8:35.

Chapter Five

1. Barret, et al, *World Christian Encyclopedia,* Vol. 1, 11.
2. Paul J. Achtemeier, *Harper's Bible Dictionary,* 1st ed. (San Francisco: Harper & Row, and Society of Biblical Literature, 1985), 287 (emphasis mine).
3. Vine, et al., Vol. 2, s.v. "Money (love of)," 415.
4. J. D. Douglas, *New Bible Dictionary* (Wheaton, Ill.: Tyndale, 1996, 1982), 357 (emphasis mine).
5. Matthew 6:13.
6. Merriam-Webster, Inc. *Merriam-Webster's Collegiate Dictionary*, 10th ed. (Springfield, Mass.: Merriam-Webster, 1996, ©1993), s.v., "Hypocrisy."

Chapter Six

1. John 8:11, paraphrased.
2. See 1 Peter 2:6–8.
3. John 17:19.
4. Vine, et al., Vol. 2, s.v. "Hallow," 287.
5. 1 Peter 2:9.
6. See Matthew 5:13–16.
7. When I say religion, I mean human religion—things people have come up with as ways to reach God; not ways God, through Jesus, has reached out to humanity.
8. See John 14:6; 1:14, 17; Romans 15:8; and Ephesians 4:21.
9. 2 Timothy 4:3–4 NCV.
10. See Matthew 23:27.
11. See Psalm 15:4.
12. Matthew 7:1.
13. Matthew 6:23 NIV.

14. See James 1:15.
15. See Matthew 3:10.
16. Romans 8:1a.
17. Romans 8:1b.
18. See Romans 12:2.
19. See 2 Timothy 4:7–8.
20. Matthew 25:21.

Chapter Seven

1. See Luke 7:11–16.
2. John 17:24.
3. See Psalm 78:41.
4. Romans 8:29.
5. See Isaiah 64:8.
6. See Acts 4:13.
7. 2 Corinthians 3:18.
8. Referring to Acts 2:16, where Peter told those gathered that "This is that which was prophesied" (paraphrased). Rev. Wilkerson's reference to this verse means that this is not yet the fullness of what God will be doing in these last days but merely the beginning, as it was on the Day of Pentecost when Peter spoke this verse.
9. See Romans 7:18.
10. See Leviticus 6:8–13.
11. See Ephesians 2:3.
12. See Ephesians 6:12.
13. See Ephesians 1:13.
14. See 2 Chronicles 7:14.

Chapter Eight

1. John 17:23.
2. James Strong, *Enhanced Strong's Lexicon* (Ontario: Woodside Bible Fellowship, 1996), s.v., "H8549 *tamiym*."
3. Ibid., s.v., "G5048 *Teleioō*."
4. Ibid., s.v., "G5046 *Teleios*."
5. Vine, et al., Vol. 2, s.v., "Perfection, Perfecting (noun), Perfectness," 467.
6. Philippians 3:14 TEV.
7. See Luke 6:45 NASB.
8. See Matthew 15:8.

9. See John 16:8–11.
10. James 2:20.

Chapter Nine

1. See Revelation 2:4–5; 3:15–22.
2. See 2 Timothy 2:3–4.
3. See Hebrews 5:12–14.
4. See Exodus 34:29–35.
5. See John 17:22–23, 25 NLT and Acts 4:13.
6. James Strong, *Enhanced Strong's Lexicon,* s.v., "H7503 *raphah*."
7. Strong, *Enhanced Strong's Lexicon,* "G2270 *hesuchazo*."
8. See Ephesians 4:8–12.
9. See John 15:19.
10. 1 Thessalonians 5:17.

Chapter Ten

1. See Matthew 26:6–13; Mark 14:1–9; and Luke 7:36–50.
2. John 17:26.
3. John 15:12.
4. Romans 5:5.
5. See Ephesians 5:23–33.
6. See James 1:22–25.

Chapter Eleven

1. See Matthew 25:14–30.
2. John 17:3.
3. John 17:21.
4. Ephesians 4:16.
5. John 17:13.
6. See Galatians 5:22.
7. 1 Peter 1:8.
8. John 17:15.
9. Proverbs 1:32 NASB.
10. John 17:19.
11. See John 15:1–8.
12. According to Vine's, "Christ" means "anointed." (Vine's, Vol. 2, s.v. "Christ," 101.)
13. John 17:24.
14. John 17:23.
15. See Galatians 2:20.

16. See Ezekiel 37:1–14.
17. See 2 Timothy 2:21.
18. Acts 4:13 and see John 17:22–23, 25.
19. See Acts 5:15.
20. John 17:26.
21. See Romans 5:5.
22. See Luke 17:21.
23. See Mark 16:17–18.
24. See John 14:12.
25. See John 14:14.
26. See Matthew 18:19.
27. See Ephesians 4:13.
28. See John 17:21.
29. See Ephesians 5:27.
30. 1 Corinthians 15:31.
31. John 16:7.
32. See Ephesians 4:13.
33. John 17:4 NIV.
34. See Matthew 16:24; Mark 8:34; and Luke 9:23.

Jerusalem
PRAYERTEAM

"Pray for the peace of Jerusalem" Psalm 122:6

The Jerusalem Prayer Team is an intercessory movement to *"guard, protect, and defend Eretz Yisrael until the Redeemer comes to Zion."* This prayer movement was launched in June 2002 by Mike Evans. The Jerusalem Prayer Team established the goal of enlisting one million members to pray daily for the peace of Jerusalem according to Psalm 122:6.

The Jerusalem Prayer Team was birthed out of a one hundred year prayer meeting at the ten Boom home in Holland. It ended when the family was taken to the prison camps for saving 800 Jewish lives. Three hundred prominent American leaders such as Dr. Tim LaHaye, Rev. Joyce Meyer, Dr. Pat Robertson, Mrs. Anne Graham Lotz, and thousands around the world are part of this prayer movement.

Be a part of prophecy today by joining. Membership is free. For more information, please visit our website at www.jpteam.org.

Name _____

Address _____

City _____ State _____ Zip _____

Email _____

Phone _____

Free gifts for new members.

You are not alone...

Jerusalem Prayer Team • P.O. Box 910 • Euless, TX 76039-0910

Best-Selling Author Mike Evans

Everything you will ever need to know, or be asked about this subject is in this book with biblical references to back it up. This classic will give you the ability to be a blessing, and to give an answer for what you believe. (I Peter 3:15)

The spotlight of Heaven is still on the Jews. Heaven and earth met there, and will meet again. The destiny of America and the world is tied to Jerusalem. The title deed belongs to God. God's prophetic time clock has been set on Jerusalem time. God promises blessings for those who pray for the peace of Jerusalem. And, Israel is the only nation of which God said, "I will bless those who bless thee."

To order Mr. Evans' book today, please send your check or money order to:

Jerusalem Prayer Team
P. O. Box 910
Euless, TX 76039-0910

Single copies: $15.00
2 to 5 copies: $13.00
6 to 10 copies: $11.00

For orders in larger quantities, please call 1-800-825-3872.

Name _____

Address _____

City _____ State _____ Zip _____

Email _____

Phone _____

Credit Card # _____

Expiration Date _____ Quantity Ordered _____